THE DIALOGUES  THE GROUP

Lacanian Perspectives on the Psychoanalytic Group

Macario Giraldo

KARNAC

First published in 2012 by
Karnac Books Ltd
118 Finchley Road, London NW3 5HT

Copyright © 2012 to Macario Giraldo.

The right of Macario Giraldo to be identified as the author of this work has been asserted in accordance with §§ 77 and 78 of the Copyright Design and Patents Act 1988.

All rights reserved. No part of this publication may be reproduced, stored in a retrieval system, or transmitted, in any form or by any means, electronic, mechanical, photocopying, recording, or otherwise, without the prior written permission of the publisher.

British Library Cataloguing in Publication Data

A C.I.P. for this book is available from the British Library

ISBN 978 1 85575 867 4

Edited, designed and produced by The Studio Publishing Services Ltd
www.publishingservicesuk.co.uk
e-mail: studio@publishingservicesuk.co.uk

Printed in Great Britain

www.karnacbooks.com

CONTENTS

ACKNOWLEDGEMENTS   vii

ABOUT THE AUTHOR   viii

SERIES EDITOR'S FOREWORD   ix

INTRODUCTION   xiii

PART I

CHAPTER ONE
Jacques Lacan 1901–1981   3

CHAPTER TWO
The other *in* the group and the other *of* the group: 9
two basic dialogues

CHAPTER THREE
"The subject supposed to know" (*Le sujet suppose savoir*)   24

CHAPTER FOUR
What happens in the venerable halls   34
of language when there is no space for the word

vi   CONTENTS

CHAPTER FIVE
From need, through demand, to desire   44

CHAPTER SIX
Revolution, evolution: change and desire   51
Part one: vicissitudes of the imaginary in the group

PART II

CHAPTER SEVEN
Revolution, evolution: change and desire   61
Part two: from identification to the desire of the other

CHAPTER EIGHT
On knowing too much   71

CHAPTER NINE
Between being and meaning: between drive and desire   79

CHAPTER TEN
Conclusion. Between an answer and a question: 91
personal musings on psychotherapy and spirituality

REFERENCES   102

INDEX   105

ACKNOWLEDGEMENTS

I would like to extend very special thanks to Professor Marshal Alcorn for his support and technical assistance.

I am also grateful to the publishers listed below for permission to reproduce/quote from previously published work.

Permission to reproduce figure "The Borromean knot" has been granted by Cengage Learning EMEA Ltd, Andover, Hampshire, UK.

In Chapter Three, the poem "Borges and I", copyright © 1967 by Grove Press, Inc., has been reproduced by permission of Grove/ Atlantic Inc.

The extract from the poem "To Julia de Burgos" in Chapter Seven is quoted by kind permission of the publishers, Curbstone Press.

The song, "Is That All There Is?", is reprinted with the permission of Hal Leonard Publishing.

ABOUT THE AUTHOR

Macario Giraldo came to the USA in 1961 with a Fulbright Scholarship to study linguistics at Georgetown University. After his MS in Applied Linguistics, he went to the Catholic University of America for his PhD in clinical psychology. He has been a member of the faculty at the Washington School of Psychiatry since 1974. He has written textbooks for the teaching of English in Colombia, as well as a number of papers and articles for academic books and journals.

SERIES EDITOR'S FOREWORD

It is with a complex mixture of pleasure, satisfaction and desire, not to say *jouissance*, that I am able to include *The Dialogues in and of the Group: Lacanian Perspectives on the Psychoanalytic Group*, by Dr Macario Giraldo, in the New International Library of Group Analysis (NILGA). The Lacanian school of thought in psychoanalysis has been neglected in Group Analysis. As Dieter Nitzgen, a leading Lacanian Group Analyst, has advised me, this book helps to address this lack. After all, we share an interest in language and the narrative, and we emphasise the importance of the "other" in nature and in the socio-cultural–political field. Lacan and even Lacanians have recognised that the unconscious is a function of both nature and civilisation, and that in the search for the lost object, mankind is always in the process of becoming. Dr Giraldo acknowledges that whereas Lacan continued to identify himself as Freudian, he was dubious about the possibility of a conflict-free area of the ego. Lacan acknowledged his appreciation of the work of Winnicott, Rickman, Bion, and other British object relations thinkers of the day. Also, Lacan's study of mirroring overlaps with Foulkes'.

Macario Giraldo would, of course, prefer to let his book speak for itself and for the value of Lacanian ideas. Yet, insight into the self of an author is an excellent bridge into the insight of his work. Therefore, I would like to tell Macario Giraldo's story in more or less his own words.

He is the ninth of ten children, seven boys and three girls, from a very simple, austere, and very well structured family of small tenant coffee farmers. His primary school was attended by boys and girls, but on alternate days, because boys worked on the farm. Some members of his family barely knew how to read and write, but his mother came from an educated family. One of her cousins was a

X SERIES EDITOR'S FOREWORD

Christian Brother from a French religious order who had become a member of the Colombian National Academy of History. He influenced Giraldo's joining, at ten years of age, the Christian Brothers, or Frères des Ecoles Chrétiennes. This enabled him to receive an education. However, he was separated from his family for four years, partly because his little village was quite far from Bogota. His late childhood and early adolescence were pervaded by a profound desire to see his parents and family, and by the agony of not being able to do this. Although he believed that it was God's wish that he join the Order and follow its rules, he was troubled by such questions as why he was not allowed to marry and have children. Years later he came to believe that such arrangements were actually criminal, and wanted to ask the Columbian Congress to forbid this custom. To this day, he wishes that he had followed his "gut wisdom".

Macario was a good student and a very good teacher of maths and languages. He won a Fulbright Scholarship to go to Georgetown University in Washington, DC to study languages. He wrote two English textbooks for teaching English at the elementary level in Colombia as part of his Master's thesis in linguistics. He lived in a religious community of the Brothers, while being groomed to become one of their leaders in Colombia. Many young people wanted him to bring to the Order the changes introduced by Vatican II. He was sent to Rome for a year of additional religious training.

Nevertheless, coming to the USA had opened his mind to completely new ways of living, new horizons, and new questions. His internal conflicts became increasingly severe. He read the books by the Jesuit scientist Teilhard de Chardin, as well as the opposition from the Vatican to these ideas. He visited a religious community in the town of Taize, and was influenced by a Protestant monk. He read Roger Garaudy's argument that essentially, for "believers" God is an answer, and for "non-believers" God is a question. Macario said to himself, "I have had the answers, but now I want the questions." He has remained a spiritual person.

In retrospect, it is hardly surprising that in the summer of 1968, having begun his studies in Clinical Psychology at the Catholic University in Washington, DC, Macario left the Christian Brothers. He had $800 in his pocket, given to him by the Order. The university helped him become a teacher of Spanish at Trinity College, and a proctor in a freshman's dormitory. He does not remember much anxiety about his economic situation. The freedom to fly, explore, and find his life was so "awesome" that he never considered the possibility that he would not "make it". In 1972, he earned his PhD in Clinical Psychology.

In 1969, in answer to his early questions about marriage and family, Macario met a graduate student in Sociology, Mabelle Riollano, from Puerto Rico. They fell in love and married in December of the same year. They have two sons, a daughter, and three "marvellous grandchildren". He says, "My family is my rock, and has amply rewarded me."

Macario has benefited from belonging to three or more cultures and being able to speak and think in several languages. He has been associated with the Washington School of Psychiatry for over forty years. The Washington School embraces pluralism in psychoanalytical theory and practice, and, at the same time, struggles with the tensions inherent in it. In fact, there is much in common between the basic ideas and values of Group Analysis and those that underpin the culture of the School, with its social and political concerns. I am pleased that Colin James, Malcolm Pines, Robin Skynner, and I introduced Group Analysis into the intellectual and clinical culture of the Washington School.

Lacan's theory is rooted in continental philosophy, linguistics, and literature, as well as in sociology and anthropology, and this informs the present text, which, after a brief, highly informative biography of Jacques Lacan, moves quickly to the issue of the "other *in* the group" and the "other *of* the group". These ideas are connected with the concept of three registers of the Symbolic, Imaginary, and Real. The reciprocal connections, restraints, and constraints of nature and society and the mind are implicitly addressed, and the importance of dialogue and discourse is emphasised. Clinical examples are deftly employed.

In reading this book, I have been stimulated to reflect on large questions about our existence as a background to our daily clinical work. I have also been able to link basic Lacanian ideas with the study of the social unconscious, and with the study of transference and countertransference processes in which it is important to work "in" the transference and countertransference and not merely "on" them. I am pleased to introduce "Mac", my friend and colleague, to the members of the mental health community who are interested in psychoanalytic group psychotherapy and, more specifically, Group Analysis, especially those who live and work outside the USA.

Earl Hopper
Series Editor

*To Mabelle Aurelia, Macario Jose, Maria Elena,
and Luis Eduardo: the anchors of my life*

Introduction

Writing this book has been a challenge. My attempt to bring the "Lacanian Freud" into the work with the psychoanalytic group is now ten years old. During these past ten years, I have conducted multiple workshops and two-day institutes, applying Lacanian theory to my work with the psychoanalytic group. To translate Lacan into the work with the group is not easy. Any translation, and especially with Lacan, implies some betrayal. Lacan, as anybody who tries to read him will attest, is not an easy author. However, I have to say that no other psychoanalytic writer has infuriated me more, and, at the same time, inspired me more, than Jacques Lacan.

In studying Lacan and in trying to translate his concepts into the work with the psychoanalytic group, I have gained greater appreciation for the extraordinary invention of what we call the psychoanalytic group. I think that this is still a very much unexplored goldmine. As the world evolves, the time to be human and personal seems to become more and more compressed. "Time is money." There is no time. The watch, the mobile phone, the next meeting, they are all calling before we have finished with the present event. While in the group, many of our patients can slow down and reconnect with their humanity. The psychoanalytic group appears as a protector of both the

xiii

xiv   INTRODUCTION

meaning of the social and the small community, and of the relevance of the unconscious, as discovered by Freud.

Lacan, of course, is not a group analyst. However, he was deeply impressed by the work of Bion and Rickman. He spent five weeks in the UK as the war was ending, and in his article, "British psychiatry and the war" (1947), he clearly expressed his respect for the work of these two pioneers in applying psychoanalysis to the work with the group in a military hospital. He writes,

> The war left me with a keen sense of unreality under which the whole of France had lived the war from beginning to end. I am not aiming here at those fairground ideologies which rocked us from the phantasmagorias of our grandeur—akin to the ramblings of senility or even the delirium that precedes death—to those compensatory fabulations proper to childhood. I would rather speak of the systematic misrecognition (*meconnaissance*) of the world by each individual, namely, those imaginary refuges that as a psychoanalyst I couldn't fail to identify in the group, prey as it was at that time to a truly panicked dissolution of its moral status, as being the self-same modes of defense that the individual makes use of against anxiety in neurosis, and with no less ambiguous a success, being just as paradoxically effective, and in the same way, alas, sealing a destiny which is transmitted to generations. (p. 9)

He adds, referring to Bion and Rickman's article, "Intra-group tensions in therapy, their study as the task of the group", that it

> will mark a historic date in psychiatry. . . . the authors bring us a concrete example of their activities in a military hospital which, with the unadorned clarity it casts on both the occasion and the principles of the said activities and with perfect humility, I would add, takes on the value of a demonstration of method. I find in their work something of the miraculous feeling of the initial stages of the Freudian elaboration: that of finding in the very impasse of a situation the vital force of an intervention. (p .15)

I discovered Lacan late in my professional life, in the summer of 1994 in Paris. I had the good fortune of hearing about Lacan, the psychoanalyst, before I knew anything about Lacan, the man. I was asked by the Washington School of Psychiatry to co-chair with Dr Justin Frank a week of conferences and study in Paris for students of the school in the Object Relations Theory and Therapy Training Program. Our interest was to establish contacts with French analysts representing important contributions to the theory and practice of psychoanalysis. Dr Joyce McDougall was both a key presenter and our co-ordinator in Paris for the conference. She invited a number of analysts, among them Jean Max Gaudilliere and Francoise Davoine, two Lacanian analysts.

I found Drs Davoine and Gaudilliere's presentations inspiring and original. They were the first to introduce me to some of Lacan's concepts. These two gifted scholars and members of the teaching faculty at the Ecole des Hautes Etudes in Paris opened for me a view of psychosis that integrated the important contributions of Winnicott, Sullivan, and Lacan with their own expanding ideas and research.

In their book *History Beyond Trauma* (2004), they provide an example of this orientation:

> Our work brings into existence zones of nonexistence wiped out by a powerful blow that actually took place. But whatever the measure chosen for erasing paths and people from memory, the erasures, even when perfectly programmed, only set in motion a memory that does not forget and that is seeking to be inscribed. In Greek, non-forgetting is, literally, *a-letheia*: This is the very name of truth, at stake in this specific memory as in the scientific approach. Hence we do not have to choose between the minute detail and the global fact. Sometimes a fit of madness tells us more than all the news dispatches about the left-over facts that have no right to existence. (p. xxvii)

This new interest has been fostered and supported in a very special way by the Washington School of Psychiatry, where I have studied and taught for the past forty years. Being a member of the faculty of the Group Program and the National Group Psychotherapy Institute has been a very rich experience for me. From the conferences that we organise each year and the intense learning and challenge opportunities that we give ourselves and our students, I have derived many lessons. Working with the members of our faculty and with gifted clinicians from the USA, Canada, and the UK has introduced me to different styles and orientations of great value. My effort in writing this book responds in large part to the interest generated in me as a consequence of these many years of continuing education in the Washington School of Psychiatry.

xvi INTRODUCTION

If I look deeper into the motivating forces behind these essays, I am fairly clear that they come from my original large family group, my present family, my patients, and my students.

My cross-cultural experiences from the countryside of the Andes of Colombia, through a kind of cultural exile lasting more than twenty years, and then coming to the USA have given me something that I find difficult to put into words. When I speak of cultural exile, I, of course, do not mean to say that an experience of that kind is not meaningful. On the contrary, I think that that put the seeds in me of a powerful desire for and of the group. For the one in exile, the group left behind and the new group might become a trilogy of the group that was, the group that could have been, and the group that was not. This kind of trilogy is at the level of the social, a powerful stimulus for a small community that feeds a desire continuing to reappear and disappear, to repeat in some way, perhaps, the lost group of paradise, where the Almighty, the first couple, and the serpent seemed for a while to live in harmony.

Some of the chapters of this book are derived in part from presentations at the Washington School of Psychiatry and at the American Group Psychotherapy Association (AGPA) and from previously published articles. Chapter One is a more detailed presentation of Lacan's personal and professional history than the short summary one often encounters in some books. I have been guided in this summary primarily, but not only, by the English translation published by Columbia University Press (1997) of Elizabeth Roudinesco's biography of Jacques Lacan. Because not many clinicians in the USA are familiar with Lacan, I thought it useful to present a few aspects of his life that might throw light on his work as psychoanalyst and thinker.

Chapter Two is an introduction to Lacan's Imaginary and Symbolic, and how they inform my concepts of dialogues in the group and dialogues of the group.

Chapter Three addresses Lacan's concept of the Subject Supposed to Know, the analyst in the analysand's view, and how this position given to the analyst by the analysand informs the transference.

In Chapters Four and Five, I use a vignette from a group session that took place years before my exposure to Lacan. This retrospective view is intended as a bridge between my object relations approach of that time and my new reading of the group through a Lacanian orientation. These chapters also present the linguistic foundation of Lacan's formulation of the unconscious.

Chapters Six and Seven are expansions and modifications of an article I published in *Group Analysis*, 34(3) in September of 2001. From the dynamic process of two small groups that merge into one new group, I point out aspects of the work with the two basic dialogues, the dialogue *in* the group and the dialogue *of* the group. Lacan's three registers of Symbolic, Imaginary, and Real are presented within the clinical material.

In Chapters Eight and Nine, I use the clinical material from a couples' group session to further examine the group dialogues in the light of Freud's concept of drive and desire as expanded by Lacan. Distinctions between drive and desire, being and meaning, jouissance and the subject of speech, and between the Cartesian subject and the Lacanian subject are introduced.

These chapters are not meant as a full elaboration of these very central and difficult concepts. They are introduced within the clinical material in a very preliminary form to give the clinician a starting point in an orientation that can be deepened by further study and reading of Lacanian literature.

Chapter Ten is again an expansion of a paper I presented at the AGPA in Boston in 2001 as member of a panel exploring spirituality and group psychotherapy. In it, I link desire and the Real as a form of spirituality for the clinician. Two vignettes, the first from the autobiography of the English mathematician and philosopher Bertrand Russell and the second from the sudden and tragic death of a group member, are presented.

In this book I present a number of perspectives using central Lacanian concepts to invite the clinician into a different reading of the group therapy phenomena.

I consider my effort as just the beginning of a process that can further help to discover and elaborate the Freudian/Lacanian concepts for the advancement of group psychotherapy. If anything, I would like to plant the seeds of an attitude that can deepen the understanding and practice of group psychotherapy by inviting the clinician to rediscover the talking cure in the group as a cure that requires a close and deep attention to the use of language in the group.

This book is intended as a friendly yet serious invitation to group therapists to take the challenge and begin to wrestle with Lacanian concepts as they look at the group. The book is not meant as an organised, systematic exposition of Lacanian theory as applied to the group. Neither does this book present a systematic guidance to technique as modified by a Lacanian orientation. In a sense, the book is more a sampling of appetisers at the psychoanalytic table for the clinician to develop a unique taste, if you will, for the Freudian discovery as expanded by Lacan. What Lacan has done is to rescue the central message of Freud and build on it a new reading for psychoanalysts and therapists. It is a view that has invigorated the psychoanalytic field and opened it to the human sciences in contemporary culture.

As I have been applying a Lacanian model to my ongoing groups, I have been developing forms of intervention that, although still faithful to some degree to what I learnt from object relations and self psychology, at times greatly differ from those theoretical roots. My hope is that in future publications I can become more explicit on technique in the application of Lacanian concepts to the group.

To conclude, for those who start cultivating these ideas as they listen to the group dialogues, I wish them the joy and excitement of the new horizons that have opened up for me in the last few years since I became acquainted with Lacan. I have benefited a great deal from the Freudian/Lacanian orientation to the unconscious in the group. The way I listen to the stories in the group, and the ways the group members learn to listen to each other and the therapist, have translated into a significant shift in both my theoretical approach and therapeutic technique. The storyteller more than the stories, the subject more than the ego, begin to appear in the group dialogues, and the resolution of the transference is, I believe, greatly facilitated. When empathy in the group moves from primarily a recognition of each other's semblances to the humbling realisation and acceptance of a basic human lack and an unbearable knowledge informing the human subject, both the therapist's role and the group members demands on each other begin to lose their powerful grip on the group. The possibility is opened for each member to become more responsible for his/her desire and for the tolerance and enjoyment of our ineffable rediscovered ignorance, transformed now into an active *savoir*.

PART I

CHAPTER ONE

Jacques Lacan 1901–1981

Both Freud and Lacan came as psychoanalysts to visit the USA. Freud presented a view of man that was revolutionary. For America, the land open to new ideas and enterprises, his views were first welcomed. But Freud's message militated against our tendency to idealise the human condition. In an important sense, his psychoanalytic project represented a critique of America's assumed role as healer of the world's wounds.

Over the years, Freud's message has been devalued or at least considered outmoded. In recent years, Jacques Lacan's "return to Freud" has been gaining ground in the USA.

Lacan sought to preserve the basic contributions of the founder of psychoanalysis. For Lacan, the talking cure and the unconscious are intimately connected to the laws of language. It is not surprising, perhaps, that in the USA it is through the fields of literature, philosophy, literary criticism, and gender and film studies that Lacan has gained recognition rather than through traditional psychoanalytic institutes.

Yet, it is clear that Lacanian psychoanalysis is gaining ground in many clinical circles in this country. Perhaps time is ripe for a return to Freud. Lacanian psychoanalysis could certainly operate as a powerful

4 THE DIALOGUES IN AND OF THE GROUP

antidote to the trend in our society to deny the importance of the unconscious by assuming a technico-scientific model of the human.

This quick look at Jacques Lacan's life might serve as an introduction for those clinicians who are just beginning to familiarise themselves with his contribution to our field.

It is my hope that by learning about Lacan, the man, the psychoanalyst, and the thinker, the reader might feel invited to take the journey through these pages where I begin to apply Lacanian concepts in my work with the psychoanalytic group.

Jacques-Marie Emile Lacan was born in Paris 1901. He was the first child of Alfred Lacan and Emilie Baudry. In 1902, a brother, Raymond was born, and died two years later of hepatitis. A sister, Madeleine Marie Emmanuelle was born in 1903 and eventually, after marrying, went to live for many years in Indochina. Another brother, Marc-Marie (later Marc-François) was born in 1908. He later became a Benedictine monk at the Abbaye de Hautecombe. On Lacan's mother's side the ancestors had been vinegar merchants, while his father's family had been in the grocery trade. Jacques ("Jacquot" in his early family environment) had a special relationship with this brother, called "little Marco". Jacques helped Marc in school and, as Roudinesco points out, acted very fatherly towards him.

According to Roudinesco, "Jacques' memory of his childhood in that apparently normal and conventional family was terrifying" (p. 8). There were constant squabbles within the family and he particularly despised his paternal grandfather, Emile, whose name he had and who was despotic towards Jacques' father, Alfred, and towards Jacques. Marc wrote that this grandfather played a more important role than Alfred did in Jacques' concept of the *name-of-the-father*.

Jacques went for his secondary education to the well-known college, Stanislas. This was a traditional French Catholic institution where the well-to-do sent their gifted progeny. Charles de Gaulle and other important public figures passed through their halls before the First World War. From 1917–1918, one of his teachers was Jean Baruzi, a rationalistic Catholic thinker. During that time, he also discovered the writings of Spinoza, a philosopher who influenced Lacan for the rest of his life. Roudinesco states that Lacan's character was not pleasant to teachers, who even feared him. He was sarcastic and furiously competitive with his peers. In 1915, his father was called up to serve in the First World War and the College Stanislas was partially converted into a military hospital for soldiers wounded at the front. Roudinesco wonders if "it might have been the sight of these men, with their missing limbs and dazed expressions, that made Jacques want to be a Doctor" (p. 10).

Lacan finished his secondary education in 1919; after a brief stay in the military, he was discharged because of his thinness. He then went into medical school and, by 1927, began his clinical training in psychiatry.

In 1929, his brother, Marc, joined the Benedictine monastery at Hautecombe. This was a very difficult and sad moment for Jacques. He had done everything in his power to prevent his brother from taking this course. He had already rejected his faith and religious upbringing, reinforced by his reading of Nietzsche. In 1935, he attended Marc's ordination as a priest but never went back to Hautecombe after that.

By 1931, he was becoming immersed in surrealism. During this time he met Salvador Dali and had his first encounter with the woman he was to call Aimee, a patient at the Hôpital Sainte Anne. He used her as a case to demonstrate his theory of paranoia, and published his doctoral dissertation in 1932: "On paranoiac psychosis in its relations to the personality". By now, his extensive knowledge of philosophy and psychiatry was leading him to attempt a synthesis of clinical psychiatry, the teachings of Freud, and surrealism. Salvador Dali praised Lacan's thesis: "Because of it we can for the first time arrive at a complete and homogeneous idea of the subject, quite free of the mechanistic mire in which present-day psychiatry is stuck" (quoted in Roudinesco, 1997, p. 60).

Alexandre Kojeve began lecturing on Hegel's *Phenomenology of Spirit* at the Ecole des Hautes Etudes in 1933. Lacan attended regularly for the following years. Kojeve taught Hegel to a whole generation of French intellectuals. Kojeve and Lacan were planning to do a study entitled "Hegel and Freud: attempt at a comparative interpretation". Although the project did not materialise, Roudinesco points out that from Kojeve's writings "there are three major concepts that would be used by Lacan in 1938: The I as subject of desire, Desire, as the revelation of the truth of being, and the Ego, as the site of delusion and the source of error" (p. 106).

In June 1932, Lacan entered analysis with Rudolph Lowenstein, at the time an authority in the SPP (Societé Psychanalitique de Paris),

6 THE DIALOGUES IN AND OF THE GROUP

who would eventually emigrate to the USA because of the Second World War, and who would become, with Heinz Hartman, a key figure in the development of ego psychology.

By 1934, Lacan joined the SPP as a candidate member. The same year he married Marie-Louise Blondin, with whom he had three children: Caroline, Thibaut, and Sibylle. By 1941, he had a daughter, Judith, by Sylvia Bataille, estranged wife of Georges Bataille. That same year, Marie-Louise requested a divorce. Lacan eventually married Sylvia in 1953, and, that same year, became president of the SPP.

Lacan's analysis with Lowenstein lasted more than six years and was a rocky one.

Kojeve and Lowenstein became for Lacan two very different influential relationships. From Kojeve, according to Roudinesco,

> The second great theoretical renovation carried out by Lacan, which led him from his already Freudian reading of psychiatry to a philosophical reading of Freud, originated in the plan for a two-handed collaboration, a partnership in which the mentor in Hegel to a whole generation brought the ideas of his pupil within the sphere of a vast phenomenological whole, centered on such Hegelian–Freudian questions as desire, the cogito, self-awareness, madness, the family, and the illusions of the ego. (p. 106)

By 1944, Lacan was an established member of a group of Parisian intellectuals, writers, artists, and philosophers. He was invited to meet Sartre, Beauvoir, and Camus during a public reading of Pablo Picasso's 1941 play, *Desire Caught by the Tail*. This social event was happening during the dramatic historical time when Paris waited eagerly for the Allied landings.

In September 1945, Lacan spent five weeks in England. He devoted close attention to Bion's new ideas about groups and to his modifications of Freudian theory. He had already been influenced by his friend, George Bataille, who had founded in France the Group Psychology Society on the basis of Freud's ideas. Lacan thought that Bion's group experiments in the mental hospital at Northfield underscored the necessity of modifying Freud's emphasis on the identification with the leader. The British clinician's successful work with many of the soldiers indicated to him an important shift to the horizontal identification with fellow group members. "Thus in 1945 Lacan was praising the English democratic system for having incorporated Freudian theory into its way of thinking and then having used it as a weapon against fascism" (ibid., p. 175).

From 1959 to 1964, Lacan's ideas on training analysis and his practical implementation of important theoretical constructs in his work with patients led him to a state of war with the International Psychoanalytic Association (IPA). Already, in 1953, following his election in January as president of the SPP, a split developed between medical and non-medical factions. Lacan was very much in favour of accepting non-medical candidates. In June of the same year, Lacan resigned and, with his followers, formed a new professional association, the Societé Francaise de Psychanalyse (SFP). On 26 September of the same year, he presented in Rome his famous paper, "Fonction et champ de la parole et du langage en psychoanalyse" (Function and field of speech and language in psychoanalysis), also called the discourse of Rome.

In 1959, the SFP applied for formal affiliation with the IPA. In 1961, an IPA committee answered with a number of recommendations, effectively demanding the exclusion of Lacan and his closest followers from SFP training programmes. In 1963, the SFP voted on the IPA's recommendations and Lacan was forced to leave the association. On 21 June 1964, Lacan founded a new psychoanalytic school and society, the Ecole Française de psychanalyse (EFP), its name was changed soon to Ecole Française de Paris (EFP).

Lacan described his exit from both the IPA and his own SFP as an "excommunication". However, his teaching was welcomed by others in key positions, such as the historian Fernand Braudel and the Marxist theoretician Louis Althusser. Soon, Lacan's seminar continued in the distinguished halls of the Ecole Normale Supérieure. His audiences increased now to include students of philosophy, literary criticism, and the human sciences. Among them was Jacques-Alain Miller, who was to marry Lacan's daughter, Judith.

Lacan travelled to the USA twice, in 1966 taking part in a symposium at Johns Hopkins University, "The languages of criticism and the sciences of man", and in November and December of 1975 lecturing at Yale University, Columbia University, and the Massachusetts Institute of Technology.

In January 1969, a Lacanian department of psychoanalysis was founded at the new University of Paris-Vincennes. By then, Lacan's

8   THE DIALOGUES IN AND OF THE GROUP

teaching had become known to a much larger audience, and he was very influential in the student–worker revolution of May 1968 that almost brought France to a standstill. This led to a demand for him to leave the Ecole Normale Supérieure, but again, he was welcomed, this time at still another grander amphitheatre, the Faculté de droit near the Pantheon, where he continued his teaching.

In 1979, Lacan co-founded with his daughter, Judith, the Fondation du Champ Freudien as a Lacanian institution separate from the EFP. His problems with institutions continued to the very end of his life. He stepped in to take charge of the department of psychoanalysis at the new university and, in 1980, unilaterally dissolved the EFP. In October 1980, he founded the Ecole de la cause freudienne and appointed Jacques-Alain Miller to a key position, making him effectively his successor, in addition to being his literary executor.

He travelled to Caracas, Venezuela, to open the first international congress of the Champ Freudien. He died the following year, 1981 after a long struggle with abdominal cancer.

Lacan's influence at present is not diminished; on the contrary, it is on the rise. Slowly but surely, even in the clinical arena, where his reworking of Freud in the USA had been largely ignored, it is beginning to appear strong and fresh in small groups in quite a few cities, such as New York, Boston, Buffalo, Philadelphia, Miami, Boca Raton, Pittsburg, Chicago, Atlanta, San Francisco, Omaha, Washington, DC, and a few others.

Social theory, feminism, gender studies, literary theory, and film theory have been greatly stimulated by his ideas. Whether there is agreement or disagreement with his basic ideas, respected scholars in all of these disciplines are using Lacan's ideas in developing applications of psychoanalysis to the critical understanding of these fields of enquiry in ways not seen before.

As Homer (2005) points out,

> By the late 1970's [sic], psychoanalytic theory had largely fallen into disrepute within the universities. Psychoanalysis was particularly criticised for its reductionism, that is, reducing all social and cultural phenomena to psycho-sexual explanations. Whatever else one thinks about Lacan and his influence, the force of his 'return to Freud' has been to make us reconsider the relationship between the unconscious and culture, between the psyche and the social, in radically new and innovative ways. (p. 111)

CHAPTER TWO

The other *in* the group and the other *of* the group: two basic dialogues

As the group members come together with their therapist for the analytic session, they either begin to talk about themselves, address one another, or remain silent. The therapist listens and at certain times makes comments. All of us practising psychoanalytic group therapy are familiar with this most marvellous of ordinary meetings.

In applying the Lacanian lens to this process, I look at the group as engaged in two dialogues within the transference. In the first dialogue, the dialogue *in* the group, people react to one another and to the therapist from a position in the transference that Lacan would call Imaginary.

What is meant by this is not that the communication is not real from a conscious point of view. What is meant is that the group members try to establish a position in the group from the relationship they have to their own ego, and, consequently, this informs their view of each other and the therapist. In this formulation, the ego is seen as an object, an object that has formed from the early images of child-hood. It is the image, the visual, or what is often called the mirroring in other psychoanalytic theories, that is central in this conception of the speaker.

9

10   THE DIALOGUES IN AND OF THE GROUP

Lacan distinguishes this object, the (moi), from the subject, the (je), or I, that is not objectified but is represented by language, by the signifier, a subject that is the effect of language.

For Lacan, then, the ego does not occupy the pre-eminent position that it does for other psychoanalytic theories. Being an imaginary object, and one that alienates man from himself, what is important for Lacan is to dismantle the distortions and misrecognition (meconnaissance) that are part of its formation. This does not mean that this ego is to be avoided and have no attention paid to it. In actuality, a lot of our work in the psychoanalytic group is first directed at the dialogue *in* the group, the immediate source of conflict and pain associated with all the imaginary formations that each person brings into the group and that need to be decanted and filtered gradually to mediate communication.

Lacan began to elaborate his position on the ego at an early stage in his theoretical work. He first presented his views in his 1936 paper on the "mirror stage" at the fourteenth congress of the IPA in Marienbad (Lacan, 1949). In Seminar I, he goes so far as to say, "the ego is structured exactly like a symptom. At the heart of the subject, it is a privileged symptom, the human symptom par excellence, the mental illness of man" (Lacan, 1953–1954, p. 16).

Lacan was concerned that Freud's first theory of the mind, conscious, preconscious, and unconscious, was being neglected in favour of the structural theory of id, ego, and superego. As Evans writes, "Lacan argues that Freud's discovery of the unconscious removed the ego from the central position to which western philosophy, at least since Descartes, had traditionally assigned it" (1996, p. 51).

For Lacan, then, the ego is an imaginary formation, the product of the mirror stage, and an object that first alienates man in the image and that functions spontaneously in all our relationships.

As the group members continue to engage in conversation, I pay close attention to another dialogue that is gradually manifesting itself. This begins to appear in slips of the tongue, momentary spurts of laughter, or uncomfortable silences, agitated interventions, lateness, missed sessions, forgetting, different ways of handling the payment of fees, compulsive smiling, or annoyance, etc. Such behaviours might illustrate how what Lacan calls the "saying" as opposed to the "said" begins to filter through the ego narrative. Of central importance in attending to the unfolding of this dialogue is the use by group members of certain phrases, certain words that, unbeknown to them, begin to express the work of the repressed unconscious in the use of certain key signifiers. I call this the dialogue *of* the group.

I contrast these two dialogues with the prepositions *in* and *of* to bring attention to a central aspect of the concept of desire in Lacan. The object in desire is not the same as the object of desire. The object in desire is any object that metonymically appears in our lives and catches our longing because it connects us with the object of desire, the lost object of our earliest, full satisfaction that, according to Freud, has left a trace that retroactively becomes an object organising our search for satisfaction. This distinction is important to understand also the concept of lack intimately related to desire. Desire persists because there is a lack-in-being. There is a lost sense of oneness. There is always in the group a strong tendency to recreate this oneness at the expense of individual differences through idealisation. Through the dialogue *in* the group, the relationships of each member come into existence in the group and the horizontal transference present to all the metonymic longings of desire. Through the dialogue *of* the group, the group members are led to face a basic lack, a lack in being, an aspect of helplessness, what Freud and Lacan call castration, as the core of the human subject.

The dialogue *in* the group deals with communication, with mediation through the other. The dialogue *of* the group deals with revelation, with mediation through the Other.

How each member and the group uses language, the set of symbols through which we have become speaking beings (*parl-être*), is what Lacan calls the Symbolic. The register of the symbolic is there before the child is born. It influences the name that is chosen for the child, and it begins to mark the newborn with homogeneous cultural symbols and a unique speech numerator. The homogeneous cultural symbols become the known, accepted use of language by each cultural group. The speech numerator is the specific speech, the way how, in each family and individual, this cultural use is given an additional element of unique meaning that develops in the history of each person's family and immediate cultural surroundings. We are spoken before we speak. We are taken by language before we can choose whether to speak or not, to use this language or any other.

We are taken by an Other, by language, and made members of the social group.

The desire of our parents and relatives, but especially of our mothers, is passed on to us through our names, through the words, phrases, songs, and rhythms of early life. All of this becomes the Other and not simply the other. So, the symbolic engraves dialectically our unconscious. Speaking from the position of the ego, the said, we can echo the words of the French poet Rimbaud, "I is an other". On the other hand, by the fact that we are spoken and brought into desire by language, we can say that we come from the Other.

The third register in Lacan's trilogy is the Real. The real is not reality. Lacan used the concept of the real in different ways depending on the stage of his theoretical development. Essentially, the concept addresses that aspect of the life of the human subject that resists the action of the symbolic. The real is. In the imaginary, we deal with the look-alike, with the rival, with our semblance in the other. Through the symbolic, we establish difference and boundaries. The real has to do with impossibility and trauma. It brings us closer to the drives and, specifically, to the ways in which we come into *jouissance*. This concept might become clearer in subsequent chapters, but, at this point, it is sufficient to say that the expression "come into *jouissance*" relates to Freud's distinction, in *Beyond the Pleasure Principle* (1920g), of a death drive that goes against the life drive supported by the pleasure principle. The human encounters the voice of the parents and the ideals and prohibitions of society and responds with the drives against this action experienced traumatically against its nature. This is a basic experience of *jouissance*, of a mixture of tension, pain, and pleasure, different from the homeostatic one of the pleasure principle. In this experience, the human takes one of three positions, according to Lacan: (1) neurosis; (2) perversion; (3) psychosis.

In neurosis, there is a compromise in the symptoms between the natural man and the ideals, prohibitions, and demands of society. In perversion, the subject stays on the side of nature but is aware of the law of the father, of the impositions brought about by the symbolic. In perversion, there is an attempt to find a way around the law. In psychosis, there is a foreclosure of a central signifier, the phallus, in this case not the organ, but the signifier of desire. The phallus, in this sense, is that absent signifier, whose very absence establishes the law that comes into existence through the name of the dead father in Freud's myth of totem and taboo. The psychotic suffers a foreclosure of this signifier, whose role is to link all of the other signifiers of the symbolic system to establish the social link.

Can the real be moved to the domain of the imaginary and the symbolic? In reading Lacan, and especially as he developed this concept towards the latter part of his career, one might come away with the impression that it can happen, but to a limited extent. There is always a left-over that remains outside of the imaginary and the symbolic that resists signification in the human subject.

In the psychoanalytic group, when traumatic events are talked about and shared with others who can relate even by simply listening, a power of liberation might ensue similar to a kind of successful "exorcism". There are moments in our groups when the experience of the human that cannot be put into words acquires an unmistakable presence. Through sensations and images, something comes out of the formless state, similar to the human face out of the formless marble or stone, to receive a name, a signifier that puts man out into the symbolic and rescues the dignity of the person.

Is the experience of the real always part of the group? It is always there, present or latent. It is sometimes manifested by chronic impasses and experiences of helplessness that resist any attempt to provide relief. In this sense, I do not conceptualise this experience as a dialogue *in* or *of* the group, but, yet, it is the material on which the imaginary and the symbolic rest. There is, all the time, a necessary tension between these three registers, the imaginary, the symbolic, and the real.

How does Lacan reformulate Freud's concept of the unconscious? He takes away any biological aspect of it and, in a sense, we can say that, in Lacan, the unconscious is essentially social. On the other hand, Lacan restores the talking cure by insisting that Freud gave us plenty of evidence of how the unconscious operates through key signifiers: for example, in the specific ways, in the treatment of the Rat Man, that Freud takes him through the various associations and different significations of the signifier *ratten*, and how those signifiers tie together the Rat Man's symptoms. I find Lacan's version of the unconscious to have a great potential for group theory and work. This is one of his early formulations of the unconscious:

It is therefore in the position of a third term that the Freudian discovery of the unconscious becomes clear as to its true grounding. This

14 THE DIALOGUES IN AND OF THE GROUP

discovery may be simply formulated in the following terms: The unconscious is that part of the concrete discourse, insofar as it is transindividual, that is not at the disposal of the subject in re-establishing the continuity of his conscious discourse. (1966, 258/49)

As Scott Lee (1990) points out, commenting on this definition,

The unconscious is neither genuinely individual nor a matter of dispositions or tendencies. It is rather 'the censored chapter' of the analysand's history, and as such the unconscious is the dynamic product of the analysand and his (censoring) environment, existing positively in a variety of the analysand's essentially symbolic behaviours. (p. 44)

Miller (1996) writes that

Lacan, in a sense, transferred many phenomenological considerations to the unconscious. It was essential to him that the unconscious not be taken as an interiority or container in which some drives are found over on one side and a few identifications over on the other—associated with the belief that a little analysis helps clean up the container. He took the unconscious not as a container, but rather as something ex-sistent-outside itself-that is connected to a subject who is a lack of being. (p. 10)

These clarifications point to a view of the unconscious that is social, that takes place between the subject and an interlocutor, and not simply to a private unconscious singularly organised and dependent on biological tendencies. The former orientation implies the view that the psychogenetic origin of mental disorders must be given a central role in personality organisation.

Lacan extends these views to the larger society. In his article, "British psychiatry and the war" (1947), mentioned in the introduction, Lacan draws attention to the unconscious in the large group, comparing in this case the different response of France and Britain to the reality of the war.

Lacan spent his time in England carefully studying Bion and Rickman's experiment with the group in the Northfield centre. What he learned from his visit influenced him to such an extent that years later, in 1964, when he founded his school after leaving the IPA, he established the small group that he called cartel as a key element of the structure of his new school. The cartel has the function of evaluating the psychoanalytic candidate before becoming a member of the school. A small group of peers reports to a committee of senior analysts recommending the candidate. This was supposed to be modelled on Bion's group task, rather than on the charisma and/or hierarchical privilege of the leader.

Lacan's registers are represented as three rings linked in such a way that, if one is severed, all three become separated (1975, p. 130). These registers colour, or influence, every aspect of Lacan's theorisation. At the centre of the three rings is the place of object *a*, the object of desire, or object cause of desire, the lost object. This graph is called the Borromean Knot (Figure 1).

In applying Lacan to my work with the group, I pay special attention to another of Lacan's graphs. This is one of Lacan's most commented upon schemas, the schema L (Figure 2). We can look at this

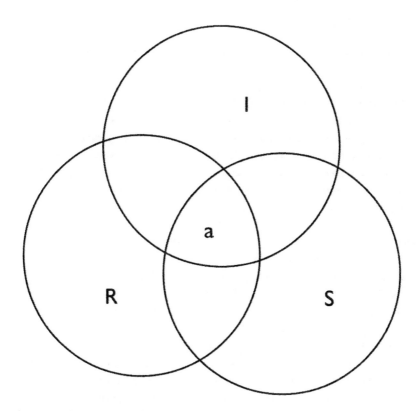

Figure 1. The Borromean knot.

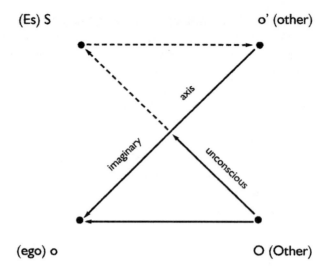

Figure 2. Lacan's schema L.

schema and begin to identify the two coexistent dialogues operating in the group.

There are four key positions identified in this schema: in the upper left corner the subject, S (Es for the sound of the first letter of the French word, *sujet*, and also the German word *Es*, it, the id in Freud); in the lower left, the ego, o. The other, o', alter ego, semblable, or look-alike, is at the top right, and the Other, O, at the bottom right, standing for the symbolic order and for the unconscious. The S for the subject is written with a bar (/) crossing the S to indicate the cut on the human, on the natural man, by the symbolic.

Between o and o' flows the imaginary dimension of the subject. Between S and O flows the symbolic dimension of the subject. The imaginary dimension is represented by a solid line from the ego to the other. The symbolic dimension is repreented by a solid line up to the middle where it encounters o–o', and then continues to S in a broken line, indicating the effects of the unconscious on the subject as the word crosses the image.

In "The mirror stage as formative of the function of the I as revealed in psychoanalytic experience" (1949), Lacan explains how the child's sense of identity is first organised by the image.

In the trajectory from the dyadic relationship to the mother to the more autonomous subject brought about by language, the child first identifies himself with an image of himself. This becomes a first organisation of otherness *vis-à-vis* mother. For this to happen, though, the mOther (or first care-taker) must mirror, reflect, and identify him/her with this image. This becomes an early form of objectification of self and other. Later on, once the child comes into language, a very different process is set in motion.

This new phase demands of that child an attempt to make sense of himself and the world around him by taking a position *vis-à-vis* mother and father. The voice of the parents and the words that carry that voice, rather than the objectified image, present a problem for the child. What does she want, to whom is her desire addressed? Where is that other person or interest that seems to take the mother in a different path from that which gives her full attention to the child?

The child must make sense of himself and the world around him by taking a position *vis-à-vis* mother and father. This position is inscribed by the voice that he/she listens to, rather than the image that is perceived. The voice is not a thing, as opposed to the image.

The child must now represent what s/he hears. This is a fundamental step. The child will invent, with the help of his/her fantasy, the object of the voice of his/her parents. These representations attached to the words and how they inform the human discourse is what Lacan calls signifiers. Signifiers are not simply words, but words that carry important representations informing one's life. The signifier becomes a presence (a representation) that stands for an absence, for something that does not exist in reality, something that cannot be perceived. Through fantasy, we represent things that we invent.

Commenting on Lacan's concept of the mirror stage, of the early ego as a beginning identity, Dor (1997) writes,

> The child recognizes himself in his own image only in so far as he senses that the other has already identified him with this image. He thus receives from the gaze of the other the confirmation that the image he perceives is indeed his. In this sense, the gradual emergence of subjectivity in the mirror stage prefigures the way in which the ego, as an imaginary construction, is irreducibly dependent on the dimension of the other. (pp. 159–160)

On the one hand, this early identification frees the child from the fused relationship to the mother and puts him/her on a path towards

18 THE DIALOGUES IN AND OF THE GROUP

subjectivity that culminates in the word, in language. But, as Dor points out, "It is precisely through this access to the symbolic that the subject relapse into the imaginary occurs, culminating in the advent of the ego" (ibid., 158–159).

We can say, then, that the child is organised as a psychic unit first by the image that comes from the other, and later by the word, the signifier, that comes from the Other. Here, Other stands for language, for the symbolic. Because it is usually the mother that initiates the child into language, it also stands for mother. The organisation by the image is the ego. The organisation by the signifier is the subject. So, whenever we read the word subject in Lacan, the signifier is implied, and it means there is a basic distinction between ego, moi, an objectified dimension of identity, and the subject, an entity that implies absence, unknown, as opposed to ego, an entity that appears as known because of the objectification in the image. This basic psychic dynamic between image and signifier, between ego and subject, between objectification and lack-of-being is expressed by Lacan in *Ecrits* (1966) as "the drama of the subject in the word is that it is there that he puts his lack-of-being to the test" (p. 655).

When I, as a subject at S (see Figure 2), address another subject at O, automatically I fall on the *moi*, the ego, the first holder of identity and cohesion; and, instead of addressing a true subject at O, I end up talking to someone that mirrors me in some way, an other, o', that is an alter ego, more than a true other subject. This basic dimension from ego to other (o–o') is Lacan's imaginary register. It is also the dimension of reality as we construct it through our perceptions and as we live it through our daily interactions. It is founded on perceptual reality. That does not mean necessarily that this reality is illusory, simply that it is constructed out of the image that has organised it.

The dialogue *in* the group is the dialogue of the ego as understood by Lacan. This means the dialogue of semblance and identifications. In the Lacanian registers of Imaginary, Symbolic, and Real, the dialogue *in* the group becomes established primarily, but not only, in the register of the Imaginary.

The dialogue *of* the group is the dialogue of the barred subject ($) and, consequently, the dialogue of repression, the dialogue of the unconscious as conceived by Freud and expanded by Lacan. Within the three registers, it is the dialogue that is anchored primarily on the symbolic register, on the level of the big Other (O) in contrast to the dialogue *in* the group that is anchored more on the little other (o), the semblant, the ego.

The dialogue *of* the group brings out also the signifier of desire. It is through the signifier that the desire of the Other has been grafted on the subject.

In group therapy, people come in as one of the many. They get to know each other, one by one, as one of a few. Through the horizontal transference, they begin to express the semblances of the ego and join in the ways of *jouissance*. These ways include the enjoyment of fellow human beings and also the sharing in styles of suffering of the human being. It is through this dialogue that each member begins to relate in the group. This is another way to understand the dialogue *in* the group. Group members try to establish a common ground on the basis of their relation to the ideals and prohibitions as established by their families of origin and their particular social group (the Other). Gradually, they begin to recognise their individual modalities and how they are manifestations of their family and social environments.

Through the vertical dimension of the transference, the transference to the analyst, group members assume a place that is guaranteed by the role of the analyst. The role of the analyst has to do with the task of the group. They will use this role to arrive at the reality of being divided subjects, divided between image and symbol, between conscious and unconscious.

This place becomes a sort of mental geographical location for each member, an address within the group that he/she can begin to use as an analytic home base.

This vector to the analyst gradually applies as well to the relation to fellow group members as co-analysts engaged in the same task. This vector is designed to lead the group as a whole, and each individual, to the differentiation between the Imaginary and the Symbolic, and to identify the fantasy styles through which members begin to relate in the group. The group members need the analyst as the central point of reference for their mental representations as they unfold in relation to each other and the analyst.

The fantasy styles expressed in the symptoms are theorised by Lacan as forms of "enjoyment", of *jouissance*. *Jouissance* is informed by the Thing (the unrepresentable) and by the representations of each subject. *Jouissance* implies enjoyment or suffering, and, most of the time, both combined. Eventually, the goal of the group and its

20   THE DIALOGUES IN AND OF THE GROUP

members is to lead each other, one by one, to the lack of being as fundamental to the revelation of how each one and the group organises *jouissance* in the attempt to confront a basic human drama of having *vs.* being. In this process, called the dialogue *of* the group, the members unravel the metaphoric and metonymic objects of desire they have become attached to as manifestations of the basic object of desire that Lacan calls object *a*, object cause of desire, the lost object of early life, retroactively invented to attempt to recapture this lost object.

I have chosen the two concepts, relate and use, from Winnicot's seminal article, "The use of an object and relating through identifications" (1971), because they match in many ways Lacan's Imaginary and Symbolic, respectively, as I apply them to the group.

As an example, the so-called borderline patient is one who, while in the group, cannot find that mental home base address. It is a patient who can relate only to fellow group members and the analyst, but cannot use the group. Such patients are held hostage by the imaginary and can hold the group hostage to this reduced dimension where words do not yet have the power to bring them out more fully into the symbolic register. It is the capacity that each member has for object use that will contribute directly to his/her capacity to learn to use the group as a therapeutic instrument.

Those patients that cannot use the object will relate intensely to the group members and to the analyst, but will remain limited in their capacity to use the group therapeutically. In other words, they are very limited in developing the dialogue *of* the group and, instead, they practically overwhelm, at times, the dialogue *in* the group and can put the analyst and the group members to the test as to how to maintain the psychoanalytic culture that is guaranteed by the symbolic in the dialogue of the group.

In *Freud as Philosopher* (2001), Boothby compares Lacan's Imaginary and Symbolic registers to Freud's concepts of "thing-presentation" (*sachvorstellung*) and "word-presentation" (*Wortvorstellung*) in his essay, "The unconscious" (1915e, p. 201).

Boothby writes,

> By relating the distinction between thing- and word-presentations to the two modalities of the psychical process, Imaginary and Symbolic, Lacan militates against a crude reification of Freud's concepts. When

repression occurs, it is not because an entity called a thing-presentation is split off from the complex of an idea and cast into the pit of the unconscious, as if word- and thing-presentations could be taken as two separable halves of the body of an idea. On the contrary, repression occurs in the conflictual interplay of two essential psychical functions. It corresponds to a shift of valence from the symbolic to the imaginary axis. The unconscious is therefore not a state but a process, not a receptacle into which an idea might be closeted away but rather a kind of cross-wiring of functions in which an idea is structurally transformed. (pp. 83–84)

Lacan, in Seminar II (1954–1955), compares the dynamic interactions of the symbolic and the imaginary to the passage of electrons in a vacuum tube (Figure 3). In this figure, the transmission of data from the unconscious, the flow of primary processes, can be interrupted, distorted, bent, in the same way that the beam of electrons is affected by a second current directed across its path. Lacan says (1954–1955),

That is what's important in the schema which gives complexity to the system by introducing into it the imaginary as such. We rediscover the little optical schema . . . in the theory of narcissism. It places the perception–consciousness system where it belongs, namely at the heart of the reception of the ego in the other, for all imaginary references of the human being are centered on the image of the fellow human being.

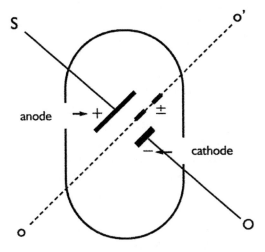

Figure 3. Lacan's schema for the interactions of the symbolic and the imaginary.

22 THE DIALOGUES IN AND OF THE GROUP

He adds,

> But above all it shows that there is not the slightest sense of relation of the ego to the discourse of the unconscious—this concrete discourse in which the ego bathes and plays its function of obstacle, of interposition, of filter—being one of negative to positive. The unconscious has its own dynamic, its own flow, its own paths. It can be explored according to its own rhythm, its own modulation, and its own message, quite independently of whatever interrupts it. In *Beyond the Pleasure Principle*, Freud wanted to situate this imaginary function of the ego. (p. 120)

The dialogues *in* the group and the dialogues *of* the group correspond, then, to two very different psychical processes. As the group dialogues evolve, the Imaginary brings the body of the group and of each member into the foreground, while the Symbolic remains more in the background. The Imaginary announces the body of the subject in the group. It might even proclaim, sometimes in the most eloquent of ways, that the body has been violated, overexcited, turned invisible, or stepped upon without the boundary of respect due to it as the being of the subject. In this sense, the dialogue *in* the group brings the being of the subject into the foreground of the group with the power of feelings. The signifier, on the other hand, through the dialogue *of* the group, brings the meaning of the subject in the unfolding of the symbolic dialogue where the desire of the subject is hidden in the word.

A psychoanalytic group might appear with a body that is sensuous, sexual, ill, angelic, or imprisoned. A group without feelings is anorexic. It feeds only from a jouissance, from an object of desire that cannot be metaphorised, decanted, or filtered, so to speak. But the Symbolic, through the dialogue *of* the group, brings the other dimension of the subject, that which protects the boundaries of the body through representation and provides its members and the group with room to breathe, to listen, to see, to wonder, and to explore. A group without the influence of the symbolic becomes a spectre. It can infantilise or traumatise its members and potentially bring paranoia. The role of the therapist in the psychoanalytic group is to maintain the focus on these dimensions, never forgetting that

> The discovery of the unconscious, such as it appears at the moment of its historical emergence, with its own dimension, is that the full

significance of meaning far surpasses the signs manipulated by the individual. Man is always cultivating a great many more signs than he thinks. That's what the Freudian discovery is about—a new attitude to man. That is what man after Freud is. (Lacan, 1954–1955, p. 122)

CHAPTER THREE

"The subject supposed to know" (*Le sujet suppose savoir*)

The French words *savoir* and *connaissance* can both be translated by the English word knowledge. *Savoir*, however, is a very different kind of knowledge from that of *connaissance*. *Savoir*, in Lacanian psychoanalysis, is knowledge that refers more directly to the drives, to what Lacan calls *jouissance*. In this sense, it is knowledge that relates more to the real. The knowledge in *connaissance* is closer to the English term. It is knowledge that is constantly influenced by the prohibitions, ideals, and laws of society, by the cultural accepted modalities of each group. It is knowledge more related to the symbolic and the imaginary. The effect of these laws and prohibitions is a gap, a lack-in-being. To this effect, as pointed out previously, the human responds with the drives and finds ways of *jouissance* as a means of circumventing the barriers imposed by the symbolic.

The drives operate through the partial objects (*breast, faeces, genitals, voice,* and *gaze*). The drive does not imply lack. Desire implies lack. The child begins to develop a way around desire to find drive satisfaction. Because some of these ways are interfered with by society, the child begins to develop forms of *jouissance* through fantasy. Through fantasy, we can go beyond the law, beyond the pleasure principle that establishes a limit to maintaining a homeostatic state in pleasure. So, *jouissance* violates these laws as opposed to the ones protecting desire.

Both kinds of knowledge, *savoir* and *connaissance*, are implied in the unconscious. The subject who comes into analysis or therapy wants to attribute all knowledge to the analyst. This is a necessary, yet a false, attribution. The analyst is on the side of *savoir*. This means that the analyst is there to assist the subject in getting to a basic *savoir*, a *savoir* that is constructed with the analyst in the treatment process. Lacan calls this the desire of the analyst, meaning that the analyst is there to lead the subject to the ways of *jouissance*, to the fundamental fantasy informing the life and the symptoms of the analysand. The analysand goes through a gradual unfolding of the main signifiers revealing the repressed desire and the fantasies that have organised the *jouissance* of the partial objects to arrive at the encounter with a fundamental fantasy where a basic *savoir* is operating, what Lacan also calls the truth of the subject, a truth the subject must confront and become responsible for. This means the subject arrives at an ethical position *vis-à-vis* himself and the world. At this point, the subject gets a glimpse of the real, and the symbolic and imaginary are modified in this encounter. This, of course, is an ideal description of the desired end of analysis. In the group, we can maintain this orientation, aware, however, that the cure might open this road for the subject, even though not everything can be accomplished during the group treatment. However, I believe there are many patients for whom the work they do in the group continues to evolve after they leave and might lead them to approach the discovery of this basic *savoir*.

In the following group session, this question of *savoir* and *connaissance* is put to the therapist. Some group members are working on how to leave the group. In the transference, one of them believes that the therapist knows of when he can leave the group. Another one is terrified of confronting this kind of knowledge and would prefer to avoid the issue completely. A third one has a dream, an example of where *savoir* comes from, and the therapist uses the dream to facilitate the dialogue *in* the group with the assistance of the dialogue *of* the group that is useful in eliciting the kind of knowledge necessary to leave the group.

This is a session from a group that has been in existence for about eight years. Most of the original members have already left treatment. In the past year to a year and a half, two people have been working

26   THE DIALOGUES IN AND OF THE GROUP

with the issue of leaving the group. They are Rodino and Brent. Rodino is in his sixties and Brent is in his late twenties. Both say that they have gone through important realisations in their therapy.

Before the start of the session, the therapist has important information about two other group members. A man, Bernie, the oldest remaining member of the group, has left a message for the therapist that he is going to leave the group. However, he has not revealed this to the group yet. He has been in the group for seven years. Another member, Yolanda, has let the therapist know that she has been involved in an exchange with the man whom she is divorcing. He called the police, and, without the proper information, the police arrested her and put her in jail for the night.

At the beginning of the group session, Donna, a forty-year-old woman, starts by saying that she has just returned from her cabin in the mountains. It was quiet and peaceful. How can she maintain some of this peace and not go back into the chaotic part of her life?

Brent says he had a strange dream. In the dream, he was checking up some kind of place, a group of people, maybe mostly women. It was a kind of cult group. Sex seemed to be somehow a part of it. It was a group that, if you signed in, you could be in for life, or for a long time, anyway.

People ask Donna about her cabin. She says that is what is left to her from a previous marriage. The therapist invites associations to Brent's dream. Catalina, very excited, giggling and having difficulty controlling her laughter, asks Brent if in the dream he tried some sexual stuff with anybody in the group. "No, I didn't," he says. Catalina's sexual desire is stimulated. She relies on Brent for the expression of her *jouissance*. But she remains estranged from her own struggle with sexuality. However, Brent's dream is useful to her gradual opening-up in the group about her sexual frustrations. Donna tells Brent that the fact that, in the dream, he was questioning whether to sign in or not confirms for her his greater ability now to evaluate issues with women. The dreamer talks now about his latest date, and how after three dates he realised that the woman did not want to start a relationship, that she was recovering from a break-up.

Brent has been somewhat awkward and unable to have romantic relations with women. He often talks about his very strong sexual drive. In his therapy, he has come gradually from a rather primitive way of relating to women to a more social attitude where he is able to talk to them not only as objects of his sexual drive, but also as people with personalities and social needs. We can say that, for Brent, the therapy has helped him gradually to experience lack, to postpone gratification, to get closer to desire.

The word cult, from the dream, attracts the attention of the therapist. The therapist and the group know that Brent has been talking for some time about leaving the group. The therapist has also in mind the phone message from Bernie telling him that he plans to leave the group. Bernie has not been able to bring this message to the group yet. He is a rather isolated man; he used to suffer from severe social anxiety in groups. He has changed in some ways, but still keeps to himself, except for his limited exchanges at work in the computer industry. The therapist knows that Bernie is having difficulty bringing to the group the message of leaving the group.

The therapist now asks Bernie, "What are your associations to the word cult?"

He responds quietly and clearly, "For me, I associate that with a group of people that put a blind faith in a leader and expect the truth from him, like a prophet, without paying much attention to their own thinking."

What the therapist does with Bernie is an example of how the material from one group member works as an association for another, one that helps Bernie overcome his resistance to telling the group that he is going to leave it. However, both members in this group will continue for a long time struggling with whether to leave the group or not, trying to get to a deeper source of knowledge that might give them the tools they need to take on a clearer responsibility for their lives.

Interpreting the therapist's question, Brent, the dreamer, says, "Now I know where you are going with that question. I think you are relating that to the therapy, to this group, how this can become like a cult. I have been saying for practically a year that I am leaving the group. Then I said, at the end of this month. Now I say it firmly (moving his hand as somebody that is drawing a line on the sand): I will leave at the end of next month, period."

The group goes then into discussing how this is not a cult. People are free to express themselves and people can leave.

The therapist now goes back to Bernie, who still has not said anything about his phone message, and asks him his thought about

28   THE DIALOGUES IN AND OF THE GROUP

Brent's interpretation. He agrees and says that it is true that some people can use the group in that way, and he wonders if he himself is really using the group well any more and that he is also thinking about leaving the group. He says it in a way that the group members listen to, but do not seem to take seriously yet.

Now the group is putting the spotlight on another group member, Paul. He is the newest member of the group. He has been in the group now for four months. He had an intense and rather difficult session the week before. He has been quiet and looking at the floor. People ask him about his job and his stress. He is able to answer a number of questions in short sentences, fairly clearly, rather than in the long and somewhat confusing verbiage of the previous week.

The older man, Rodino, tells Paul that he understands the position he is in, what he is struggling with. That sometimes one finds oneself in a kind of hole, where nothing can really alleviate the pain, and that when he has found himself in that situation he has discovered that the best thing is to acknowledge the pain and not to explain it away by not paying attention to it. Acknowledging it, he says, is often the most helpful thing. Some group members seem to act in a somewhat protective role towards Paul.

Paul says that what he wants from this group is to be listened to and for people to ask him questions, that he does not want advice (he says it rather firmly). "That would be fine in another kind of group," he adds, but it is not what he expects from this group.

Paul does not want solutions. He does not want easy identifications. He does appreciate being listened to. He welcomes the questions. They help him explore a deeper kind of knowledge.

The therapist comments that Paul's words sound very clear and there are gestures and expressions of confirmation from other group members as well.

Close to the end of the session, Rodino, also a long-standing member of the group, says that he has also been talking for more than a year about leaving the group and wants to know when. He says that what he has learnt from the group is of incredible value to him, that the most important thing is that when he came, he felt his relationship with his wife was leading him to despair. That now, as simple as it may sound, the basic difference is that the relationship is difficult, but he does not feel the despair. He looks at the therapist and asks him, "Well, what do you think?" The therapist invites him to struggle with that thought and to bring it back to the group at the following session.

Rodino does leave the group two months after this session. His basic achievement in the group is that now he does not feel the despair he used to feel. He has a problem, but it is manageable. He has brought to the group important aspects of his experience as a child in the Second World War. His wife had become repository for impossible fantasies that dated back to his first five years of life. He is more tolerant now of a lack-in-being, his wife does not have to complete him. And this has opened a new way for desire and diminished his angst to a great degree.

Then the therapist asks Yolanda, who has not said anything about her jail experience, what happened. She goes into the story, laughing and mocking the police. She was actually imprisoned wrongfully. She was considered drunk, even though she had not had any drinks, only a milkshake, and she was not tested. She made a comedy out of the whole experience, entertained the other women in jail and, actually, her ex-husband got very worried because he did not mean to take things that far.

She is somebody who is not intimidated, and somebody who has had tragic events in her life, but tends to use laughter and comedy to bypass them. The therapist felt that, for the time being, her story should not be made a central issue for this session unless she brought it out herself.

The group is momentarily surprised, and Donna, who had started the session, says now, "There is not enough time to deal with this. We need more time; time is too short. There is so much that I want to hear about." She is actually very struck by the lightness, the comic aspect of Yolanda's response, something so different from her own intense and angry outbursts when she feels misunderstood by people. At some point towards the end of this session, the therapist also announces that a young man will be joining the group. The group has been expecting new members.

Discussion

Lacan calls the analyst the subject supposed to know. He means by this that the analysand, in the transference, tends to put the analyst in

30   THE DIALOGUES IN AND OF THE GROUP

that role. However, this is not the role of the analyst. This subject supposed to know is considered in the transference as all knowing. It can be felt as a big Other, as a kind of oracle. In the constitution of the subject, language has operated as an Other. The subject has come into existence through the desire of the parents, and this desire has been communicated one way or another through language. The child's first name has a central role in this communication. The Other is language, it is the symbolic discourse. The analysand might want to get the answers from the analyst as this Other who knows, or might want the analyst to be the little other, the one like him, a look-alike, somebody who really understands him, somebody he can identify with. The role of the analyst, however, is neither as an Other nor as an other, but, rather, as somebody in the position of the object of desire, called by Lacan object (a). This object cause of desire is an object related to the early blissful satisfaction of the child–mother unit. This is a lost object. And, in reality, the word object does not quite apply, because again, in the beginning, there was only the child–mother unit, and no object. This is an object constructed retroactively. Every object that we look for, that we want to love and get love from, is only a metonymic object related to that lost object. Consequently, desire is intimately connected with a basic lack that informs our existence.

The role of the analyst is to attend to the analysand's desire, a desire that is related to a lack. In the transference, the analyst takes the place of that object that the analysand searches for. In taking this role, the analyst brings the analysand to confront his/her desire. The analyst does that by receiving the demand (or request) of the patient and in some way sustaining the patient in the struggle with that demand so that she/he can find the desire behind the demand. If the analyst rushes to respond to the demand, the patient might be deprived of encountering her lack and, consequently, her desire. That the analysand confronts his/her desire means that a certain illusion of completeness, of perfect fitting, is given up, and, instead, a certain openness to possibility and impossibility is appreciated. It also means that the analysand brings to light through the analysis the history of his/her desire and the place of the Other *vs.* the place of the subject in this trajectory.

Perhaps, in the present group session, the one member that is closer to recognising his desire is Rodino. What he says about his relationship to his wife is that now he is not in despair. He simply accepts that it is

"THE SUBJECT SUPPOSED TO KNOW" 31

a difficult relationship. He might have come to realise to some degree that there is a basic lack in both of them, and that alone might have lessened greatly his despair and anxiety. He still wants the therapist, though, to play the role of the Other, of the wise man, to agree with him on when to leave the group. The therapist invites him once more to struggle with that thought. The therapist sends him back to confront his desire as his own, and to face himself and the group with it.

The dialogue *in* the group in this particular session is centred around the issue of leaving. Two members have been working on it for an extended period of time. Another member is about to begin talking about it, but needs the help of the group and the therapist to even state his desire. For Bernie, the danger is to identify at a superficial level with the two other members and disappear from the group. The identification with the two other members that are about to leave might prevent him from confronting his desire. What is his desire? It might have something to do with separating from mother, for whom Bernie has played a very important role, but at the expense of his own autonomy. If he leaves the group through unexamined identification with the two other members, he might miss a very important part of his analytic group work. The therapist is well aware of it. The therapist will help Bernie to begin to state his desire, and will work with him and the group so that he can confront it with all the implications necessary to make his leaving a transforming therapeutic process.

The dialogue *of* the group is organised around the word cult, taken from the dream. The therapist uses this signifier to bring associations and comments from the group members on the role of the group and the therapist. The members comment on how the group could be used as a cult, and how it is not a cult, in order to bring into focus the two dialogues, and Paul, in simple terms, lets the group know what kind of group he wants. In a certain sense, this new member is asking for the dialogue *of* the group because he really wants to achieve significant realisations. Bernie, on the other hand, would like to leave still under the influence primarily of the imaginary, of the ego.

In other words, in this session the group is confronted with two kinds of knowledge about leaving the group. The first knowledge relates to a conscious knowledge, informed by the ego. Bernie is under the influence of this knowledge, which is stimulated by Brent's and Rodino's work on leaving. It is a knowledge based on identification. He feels that he is now the senior member of the group and that it is

32 THE DIALOGUES IN AND OF THE GROUP

about time for him to leave also. He wants to leave supported by a wish to join the other two members as look-alikes, as doing for him the work of separation.

There is another knowledge, however, a *savoir*, the knowledge of the unconscious. If Bernie cannot approach this knowledge, he will miss a central task of his analytic work; he will miss the information from the dialogue *of* the group. He might leave the group and the therapist as still in possession of his knowledge, rather than himself as the one confronting the knowledge of his leaving. Lacan names these two knowledges as S1 and S2. The first one is what he calls the unary signifier, the signifier that represents the subject to another signifier, S2. We can say that, in this group situation, the act of leaving operates as a first signifier, S1, which sends the subject to another signifier, S2, where the connections to the history of his desire, the unconscious elements, are hidden. The question for the group under the dialogue *of* the group becomes then: where is the knowledge necessary for the act of leaving this group? Is it in the analyst? Is it in the group? Or is it ultimately in each individual subject, informed by the unconscious?

As we all recognise, the great literary writers and poets have dealt with these issues as central to the human condition. As an example of the back and forth flow of these two kinds of knowledge and the difficulties in positioning them, we can appreciate what the great Argentinian writer, Jorge Luis Borges, says in this short prose poem:

"Borges and I"

> Things happen to him, the other one, to Borges. I stroll about
> Buenos Aires and stop, almost mechanically now perhaps, to look
> at the arch of an entranceway and the ironwork gate; news of
> Borges reaches me in the mail and I see his name on an academic
> ballot or in a biographical dictionary. I like hourglasses,
> maps, eighteenth-century typography, etymologies, the taste of
> coffee, and Robert Louis Stevenson's prose; he shares these
> preferences, but with a vanity that turns them into the
> attributes of an actor. It would be an exaggeration to say that
> our relationship is a hostile one; I live, I go on living, so
> that Borges may contrive his literature; and that literature
> justifies me. I do not find it hard to admit that he has
> achieved some valid pages, but these pages can not save me,
> perhaps because what is good no longer belongs to anyone, not

even to him, the other one, but to the language or to tradition. In any case, I am destined to perish, definitively, and only some instant of me may live on in him. Little by little, I yield him ground, the whole terrain, though I am quite aware of his perverse habit of magnifying and falsifying. Spinoza realized that all things strive to persist in their own nature: the stone eternally wishes to be stone and the tiger a tiger. I shall subsist in Borges, not in myself (assuming I am someone), and yet I recognize myself less in his books than in many another, or than in the intricate flourishes played on a guitar. Years ago I tried to free myself from him, and I went from the mythologies of the city suburbs to games with time and infinity, but now those games belong to Borges, and I will have to think up something else. Thus is my life a flight, and I lose everything, and everything belongs to oblivion, or to him.

I don't know which one of the two of us is writing this page.

(Borges, 1967)

CHAPTER FOUR

What happens in the venerable halls of language when there is no space for the word

"I never had a pet. But my sister has this little dog. I had to pick him up from the groomer. I was dressed in this white suit. As I was driving to pick him up I realised I did not have a leash. How was I going to take him and put him in the car? I did not want to mess up my suit. I have never had a pet so I never know how to handle this situation. I told the people at the clinic. They gave me this blue leash. So I put it on his neck and I was able eventually to take him to the car. So I thought: What I need is a leash, a leash to put around my neck. I have been very busy holding on to a leash for Bill and have not taken care of me. So if I can have a leash on me I'll be safe. So I was happy. I have a leash on me to keep me safe"

This is how, early in a group session, a patient entered the dialogue in the group. Her ego narrative seemed normal for a while, but gradually ended up in some alien territory. She had been recently released from the hospital after a psychotic break. She had been living in a very abusive relationship and, during the process of ending the relationship, she had a breakdown and was hospitalised. She starts her monologue by saying that this morning she had a revelation and feels very lucky. Then she goes on with the story of the pet.

The group members became very anxious. Everybody appeared momentarily disorientated. As she ended her story, this group member seemed to be in another space, a space without a contextual reference. Gradually, people began to speak. One said that she felt a knot in her stomach. Another one said that she was beginning to feel comfortable in the group and now felt she had lost that to some extent. In a subsequent individual session, a man became very angry at me, the therapist, and told me that I had betrayed him. "She is not in the group's league," he said. "She belongs to a different group of people." "How did you manage to bring her to the group?"

What was remarkable in the story was how the patient began her discourse in what appeared normal terms, with reality testing intact. Her happy, almost manic tone and delivery was, however, unusual. As she ended, she fell into a concrete phase and expressed a kind of certainty that distinguishes the psychotic discourse from regular discourse. Her demeanour at the end of her monologue was of a clear conviction: "I have a leash on me to keep me safe."

The patient was conveying in her story the elements of a *savoir*, of a *jouissance* that was destroying her life. She had been holding on to her religious, charismatic activities as a support system. But, even with her faith and prayers, she was becoming undone. Referring to her religious activities, another woman, who also came from a fundamentalist orientation, said that she "felt like vomiting from the sweet charismatic shit!" Still another man appeared quite reflective, as if he was witnessing something he was familiar with. He had experienced similar disconcerting episodes with his wife.

I was momentarily very surprised and felt a rush of anger. How could this group, usually so caring, act this way towards a member in distress?

This woman had not been that long in the group. She was still quite fragile after her release from the hospital. She was not, however, a psychotic in the sense of having a psychotic structure. The acute psychotic episode that put her in the hospital was related to a powerfully difficult decision she had made to confront her husband, her church, her faith, and the convictions that had held her hostage in her relationship. I had thought, however, that she would be able to function in a group of normal neurotics. Why was her narrative so disturbing to most of the group members?

36   THE DIALOGUES IN AND OF THE GROUP

The angry man's comment to me in the subsequent individual session, "She is not in the group's league," is an indication that something has happened in the discourse that does not fit. Does not fit what? It does not fit the agreement of a linguistic community. Yet, as the story begins, things seem to make sense. However, the word leash gradually takes on an existence of its own. And suddenly we are into alien territory, outside a linguistic agreement. "So I thought: What I need is a leash. A leash to put around my neck . . . So I feel happy. I have a leash on me to keep me safe." In Lacanian terms, the signifier leash, has lost its tie to the law of the father, to the law of language, and because of that it does not function any more as a linguistic sign. It does not stand for something, it stands on its own. The word has become concrete, it does not represent. And the anxiety in the group is a signal that the Real, not reality, is here in the group. Reality is what we construct with our imaginary and symbolic dimensions. Reality exists. We can talk about it. We share it. The real is what ex-sists, as Lacan puts it using a term borrowed from Heidegger. It is outside human reality as constructed by language.

Structural linguistics, the subject's discourse, and the unconscious

The previous dramatic and painfully touching episode is an example of the manifestations of the unconscious in language and speech. Lacan attempted, throughout his professional life, to expand to its ultimate conclusions a central point of his theory: "The Unconscious is structured like a language". He wanted to restore to psychoanalysis a more sound philosophical and scientific basis for its object of study, the unconscious. He was also concerned that both ego psychology and object relations were moving away from Freud's conceptualisation of the unconscious and this shift was changing the role of the analyst in handling the transference.

Let us use this vignette to consider some basic points that Lacan elaborated from structural anthropology and structural linguistics to give to Freud's unconscious and human subjectivity a new and more central space in the psychoanalytic map.

The linguists, Ferdinand de Saussure and Roman Jakobson, and the anthropologist Claude Levi-Strauss gave Lacan the scientific basis for his expanded concept of the unconscious taken from Freud's theory on dreams.

Ferdinand de Saussure revolutionised the study of language. He demonstrated that the linguistic sign was a relation not between an object and an acoustic image, but, rather, between a concept and an acoustic image:

Concept (signified)	s
Acoustic image (signifier)	S

There is not a one to one, natural or organic correspondence between a word (leash) and an actual object in the world. When, as English speakers, we hear the word "leash", we conjure up ideas or images of leash; they all refer to a concept and not quite to an actual, unique, individual object, leash.

So, for Saussure, the proper concern of linguistics is the *sign*, that is to say, the relation between the sound pattern or written word and the concept. They are called the signifier and the signified, respectively. Saussure used the word "sign" to indicate the whole, the relation of two terms, signified and signifier, in opposition; these terms are parts of a whole and separate from the whole.

When we speak, there is a dual flow taking place: the flow of concepts (signified) and the flow of acoustic images (signifiers). Each one of these sign units "derives its value from its opposition to all the other terms", and he compares this to the game of chess where "the respective value of the pieces depends on their position on the chessboard" (p. 88).

Saussure states that the context delimits the sign, and he gives the following example from the French language:

Acoustic image

Je l'apprends	Je la prends
(I learn it)	(I take it)

The French pronunciation is the same in both phrases. It is the context within which the sentence is embedded that will determine what the listener understands.

So, linguistic signs have meaning not simply because of their content, but mainly because of the oppositional relations between them within the spoken chain and because of the context of those signs in the discourse.

Saussure made us realise that language is a system that governs what we say and how we say it. When I say "leash" instead of rope, I am using what Saussure calls the element of selection. This element he calls the paradigmatic axis of language. But, whatever word I use, I must use it in the proper combinatory sequence, ordered by my language. I cannot say: a need I leash. I must say: I need a leash. This is the proper syntax required by the structure of the English language. This is the syntagmatic axis of language. The meaning of what we say depends not only on the choice of words, but also on the specific combination of those words in the sentence structure.

The paradigmatic and syntagmatic axis of language were expanded in their functions by the Russian linguist, Roman Jakobson (1896–1982). He demonstrated that these aspects have a correspondence with the rhetorical figures of metaphor and metonymy. In metaphor, we substitute a word for something else to which we refer. For instance, if, in the group episode, our patient had said, "I feel so constrained by Bill's demands upon me that I experience him putting a leash around my neck to go wherever he wants me to go", here the word leash would function as a substitute, a metaphoric meaning indicating the enslaving and demeaning aspect of the relationship as experienced by this woman.

In metonymy, the relation of contiguity is the important thing. The words "The White House" are associated with the office of the president of the USA. The word "sail" is often metonymically used to mean boat.

Lacan, in turn, saw in Jakobson's model a correspondence with Freud's concepts of condensation and displacement in the dream work.

In addition to the influence of these linguists, Lacan developed a close relationship with the anthropologist, Claude Levi-Strauss, whose name, more than anybody else's, is connected with what was called structuralism. What Levi-Strauss demonstrated in his studies of "primitive" societies was the existence of a basic, elementary structure governing how marriage and social relations were practiced in those societies.

From these sources Lacan arrived gradually in the 1950s to a view that what characterises the human world is the symbolic function, that before we speak we are spoken by language and that we are unconscious of the structure that governs the way we see and describe the world.

Lacan made use of Saussure's sign but made two significant corrections. For him the signifier has an autonomous quality in reference to the signified. He inverted Saussure's formula to reflect this change.

Acoustic image	Signifier	S
Concept	Signified	s

In the human discourse, the signifier is the rider, the signified, the horse.

Second, Lacan developed the concept of the anchoring point (*point de capiton*). The anchoring point is similar to that point where the upholstery (*capitonnage*) is fixed, as in a chair or a sofa. He developed this concept from psychoanalytic experience, where the relation of the signifier to the signified "always appears fluid, always ready to come undone" (Lacan, 1955–1956, p. 261). This concept of delimitation by the anchoring point is clearly manifested by its absence in the psychotic experience. He uses a schema to explain it (Figure 4).

There are two vectors: the vector of signification from D to S (from demand to the signifier) and the retroactive vector indicated by the reverse arrow that crosses the D ... S vector at two points, O and M (Other and message). This graph becomes the first stage of Lacan's graph of desire, which he went on to elaborate more extensively in

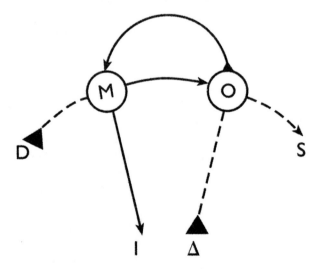

Figure 4.

40   THE DIALOGUES IN AND OF THE GROUP

later years. The retroactive vector starting at (delta) with the broken line indicates the origin of desire in pure need as it becomes caught in the circuit of the symbolic. Pure need is taken by the Other and becomes caught by the expression of Demand represented by the vector D to S. D in the chart represents demand and S represents signification. The vector from D to S, thus, represents demand as something modified by the signifier, or the symbolic. Once the mother has brought the child into the semantic universe, the desire of the child must go through the requirements of the symbolic system to attain satisfaction. The child will enter into language to "figure out" in some way the desire of the mOther, the first other that also becomes the Other. The child, thus, in its relation to this first mother, gains access to her own desire. Her demand or request becomes now the unconscious way to get to her own desire.

The signifiers of spoken chain, S. . .S', acquire meaning only retroactively. The last signifier of the chain is what gives meaning to the preceding ones. This is what the reversed direction of the anchoring vector delta to I indicates. This anchoring point "hooks" the signifying chain S. . .S' at two points. The anchoring point stops the sliding of signification.

In the patient's vignette, we can divide the discourse in the following way, indicating the beginning of the message and the end point where (O) ties the message within the symbolic:

S1	I never . . .	S2 . . .	had a pet
S3	But my sister . . .	S4 . . .	has this little dog
S5	I had to . . .	S6 . . .	pick him up from the groomer
S7	I was dressed . . .	S8 . . .	in this white suit
Etc. . . .			

As the discourse is ending, what happens is that the relation of the signifier to the signified appears fluid and comes undone.

Sn   So if I can have a leash on me . . .   Sn+1 . . .   I will be safe.

I said that the word "leash" as the story is ending has lost its metaphoric value. The word ex-ists rather than exists within regular discourse. We can see clearly the absence of the anchoring point and consequently the falling off of the previous signifiers of the story.

This ex-sistence, this outside, is the realm of the Real, of that which is not mediated by language, of that which has not been mentated. The word leash as used by the patient begins to occupy the place of an actual leash, a concrete thing. The word loses the function of representation and falls into the Referent. The word stops being part of the sign and becomes a thing.

The signifier (especially, in this case, the word leash) ends up failing to be taken up at point O (the place of the code, of the law, of the big Other) and so what is left is the message hanging in the air, not anchored by the symbolic. The message becomes a foreigner within the linguistic community. This is the ex-sistence felt in the group. This ex-sistence triggered associatively other aspects of the real in other members of the group such as: "I feel a knot in my stomach"; "I have lost my comfort (safety) in the group"; "she is not in the group's league"; "she belongs to a different group of people"; "is this my wife in the group right now?" (an experience of the uncanny).

If we go back to the previous schema L, the dimension of the Other disappears and the patient is talking from an ego to an alter ego without the backing of a third term. And, because of that, the inter-subjectivity that is present in regular discourse, thanks to the guarantee of the Other, does not function any longer. The patient ends up talking from her ego to a reflection of herself and not to another. We can say that the imaginary takes over and the group is suddenly confronted with an imaginary that collapses into the real, into the thing in itself, because the symbolic is absent. Again, if we look at Figure 4, the anchoring point does not function. It cannot tie the discourse; the message is there, but the Other (O) is not there.

In psychic structure, this Other, the symbolic, performs a central function, which works in neurosis and perversion but not in psychosis. In the latter case, this signifier, called by Lacan the paternal metaphor, is foreclosed. Consequently, its function of tying the other signifiers in the lawful required structure to create meaning and communciation fails. Although language alienates the subject from its natural being, it also rewards him or her with the advent of desire that puts the human on the road to taking a place in the linguistic, social community. In the example of this group, that function is momentarily interrupted and disrupts the group community.

42   THE DIALOGUES IN AND OF THE GROUP

The group is now in the vicinity of the real, and this, more than anything else, is what brings anxiety in the group. The group is in danger of crossing into foreign territory, yet a territory that in one way or another is part of the human experience, that psychotic part of our personality that might give way under severe stress.

The concept of the Real is associated with trauma, and with psychosis. In Lacan's late phase of development, it became intimately linked with the unconscious. Lacan's exploration of this concept put him beyond structuralism. As Homer points out,

> Lacan was not a structuralist in any strict sense of the term, however, for two reasons. First, structuralism sought to dissolve the subject completely and saw the subject as merely the 'effect' of symbolic structures. Lacan, on the other hand, while seeking to locate the constitution of the subject in relation to the symbolic, does not see the subject as simply reducible to an effect of language or the symbolic order. Second, for Structuralism, a structure is always complete, while for Lacan the structure—the symbolic order—is never complete. There is always something left over; an excess or something that exceeds the symbolic. What exceeds the symbolic is the subject and the object. (p. 65)

But where is the subject and where is the object? Lacanian theory does not answer these questions with "realistic" concepts as object relations and other forms of psychoanalytic theory do. There is an elusiveness that permeates this search. The lack-in-being confronts the subject every step of the way. However, we can use our vignette to proceed in this search. The patient had had a traumatic sexual experience in her childhood. As an adult, she had been in a relationship where she functioned as a kind of sexual pet. The discourse she brings up in the group is focused on a pet. She does not know how to handle the pet. People at the clinic give her a blue leash. She is looking for a way out of a relationship that perpetuates her early trauma. She concludes with the leash as relating to an issue of safety, liberation, and peace. Yet, she fails to arrive at a safe port, she flounders, becomes undone, the boat does not quite make it to safe ground.

What becomes a source of acute anxiety in the group is the momentary appearance of the subject and the object not veiled by the symbolic. The *jouissance* of the subject, the drives in their defiance of the demands of the symbolic, appear at *"ciel ouvert"* (open sky), using

Lacan's term. There were many aspects that could not be explored in the group at this time. The main task at the time was to maintain the role of the symbolic in order to contain the group's anxiety. The sexual trauma was communicated through a number of key signifiers: pet, white suit, leash. She continued in the group, and eventually overcame her fears of ending the relationship and went on to live a very different and more satisfying life.

Lacan says that "the signifier represents the subject to another signifier". The symbolic order represents. The subject and the object remain ungraspable. They are announced, represented. But they cannot become facts that can be measured, calculated with exactitude by the scientific method. It is in finding a *savoir*, connected to a fundamental experience of *jouissance* and the unconscious, that the subject can arrive at a position of a new choice, different from the "forced choice" imposed by the drives and the demands of the Other. This new choice implies an ethical stance *vis-à-vis* the patient's history.

I believe this was a woman who was able to arrive at this juncture. She was very courageous in confronting the structure of the Other in the way she was living, primarily under a "forced" choice. She was also able to bring out, unpack to a significant extent, the repressed signifiers connected to her *jouissance*, in her case, primarily to sexual *jouissance* related to events in her childhood. For her, the support and confrontation that the group dialogues offered her were very instrumental in the development of her ability to cross from the territory of a repressed *savoir* to a new one constructed with the assistance of her therapist and the group members.

CHAPTER FIVE

From need, through demand, to desire

The philosopher Ernst Cassirer (1946) examines the power of the unconscious syntax of experience present in culture and maintained by language in *Language and Myth*. He quotes the German naturalist and writer Alexander W. Von Humboldt, who says eloquently what language does both to and for the human being:

> Man lives with his objects chiefly—in fact, since his feelings and acting depends on his perceptions, one may say exclusively—as language presents them to him. By the same process whereby he spins language out of his being, he ensnares himself in it; and each language draws a magic circle round the people to which it belongs, a circle from which there is no escape save by stepping out of it into another. (p. 9)

We can recognise in Humbold, who preceded Lacan and the structuralists, the presence of the Other influencing our actions.

We may add that, by becoming a speaking being, the subject moves from the realm of pure need through the medium of demand or request to express the desire to and for the other.

These three fundamental steps taken by the child, from need through demand to desire, become operational in all human relations.

FROM NEED, THROUGH DEMAND, TO DESIRE   45

The group therapist's interventions and those of the group members take on a more complex meaning through the transference in relation to these three phases. The psychoanalytic concept of abstinence is tied to a proper understanding of this triad in the management of the transference. The patient will try to get to his/her desire through the expression of needs and demands that attempt to avoid the position of desire that confronts the subject with a lack-in-being. Let us at this point introduce some aspects of these concepts from Freud and Lacan.

Lacan distinguishes between need, demand, and desire. He uses Freud's 1895(1950c) work, *A Project for a Scientific Psychology*, and his later works *The Interpretation of Dreams* (1900a), and *Beyond the Pleasure Principle* (1920g), to further develop these concepts.

I will mention them here in a simplified way, following Dor's (1997) more careful and systematic elaboration. As Freud points out, at the beginning, when the child is hungry, he/she is in a state of tension and displeasure. Once fed by the mother, this first satisfaction leaves a memory trace in the brain and, as the need returns, the memory trace left over from the perceptual image of the first satisfaction is coupled with the actual present object (for instance, mother's milk) of satisfaction.

Freud adds that too great a cathexis of the mnemic image evokes a similar response as the one to the real perception of the object of satisfaction, mother's milk. This makes it possible for the child to use hallucinatory satisfaction.

When the child gets the food, and is satisfied, the mother usually adds other things, not just milk or food: the mother smiles, rocks the baby, talks to the baby, sings, looks at the baby, and holds the baby. All of these additional gifts transform what was originally a primarily physical object of need into a relationship to the other, the mother.

Furthermore, the mother, by responding to the signs of distress in the baby, has interpreted the baby's needs and referred the baby to a semantic universe where signs and symbols will become gradually elaborated into the eventual symbolic order, the law of the father. For Lacan, the mother has interpreted the child's purely physical need as a demand. From now on, the child's satisfaction takes place between need and demand, and, on the child's side, the demand is now not just for food, but also for recognition and love.

The original object of pure satisfaction was not subject to the mediation of demand. The new object of satisfaction is, and because of this, the original object in its purity is lost. The child now becomes subject to the desire of the other through demand. The child now wants to be desired by the other. The child's desire becomes, first and foremost, the desire to be desired.

The child will go on looking for the object of desire as if it were the original object of satisfaction, eternally present in the search, yet eternally absent in its finding. The child enters the incompleteness of his/her being where language will come in eventually to negotiate the absence of pure, original satisfaction and the presence of the metonymic objects of satisfaction that stand in for the lost, original object.

The construction of the object of desire functions retrospectively through demand back to need. This object of desire, called by Lacan object (a) (*objet petit a*) is then not a real object any more. What the child will look for can be met only to some degree by all those objects of satisfaction metonymically related to the original object of desire.

For Lacan, then, the object of desire speaks to the human being's basic lack, a lack of being, *manque à être*, forever subject to the Other. The desire of the Other will, from now on, shape the destiny of the drives.

Lacan places great emphasis on Freud's observations of his grandson of one and a half years of age in order to expand on the mediation of language on desire. Here is what Freud writes in Chapter II in *Beyond the Pleasure Principle*:

> The child had a wooden reel with a piece of string tied round it. It never occurred to him to pull it along the floor behind him, for instance, and play at its being a carriage. What he did was to hold the reel by the string and very skilfully throw it over the edge of his curtained cot, so that it disappeared into it, at the same time uttering his expressive 'o-o-o-o'. He then pulled the reel out of the cot again by the string and hailed its reappearance with a joyful 'da' ('there') . . . The interpretation of the game then became obvious. It was related to the child's great cultural achievement—the instinctual renunciation (that is the renunciation of instinctual satisfaction) which he had made in allowing his mother to go away without protesting. He compensated himself for this, as it were, by himself staging the disappearance and return of the objects within his reach. (Freud, 1920g, p. 15)

Lacan discusses at length Freud's observation and relates it to the function of language in the constitution of the subject. The subject, already taken by the demand of the other, which is always more than need, takes a new and more fundamental step into the symbolic. The sounds "o-o-o" and "da", as beginning words, free the child from the Imaginary dyad with his mother, alienate him through the wall of language, and leave a permanent mark of a divided subject.

In this hole, opened up by language, desire gets grafted on to the subject. The subject will be constantly trapped between what he says (the utterance) and the saying (the enunciation). As the subject speaks, he begins to be freed from the narcissistic dyad and becomes the member of a basic group, the family, and a candidate now for the human community where the laws of the group will maintain a constant tension with his desire.

The original object of satisfaction gave the child what Lacan calls a *jouissance* that became then primordially repressed when the child moved from need to demand. Now, under the repression proper, the repression of language, the object of desire will be forever hidden under an endless series of empirical objects of desire that stand in metonymic relation to the original lost object.

The object of desire, object (a), is, then, both the object cause of desire and the object we look for. The object of desire always implies absence and presence, disappearance and return, loss and encounter.

To review and apply these concepts, let us return to our group from the previous chapter, a group that was bereft and in disarray. Each member of the group, including the therapist, was then confronted with the particular dynamics of desire in this group. The group member who said, "I was beginning to feel comfortable in the group and now I feel as if I have lost that", and the one that felt a knot in her stomach, these are examples of the real, of a presence without absence, and, consequently, a presence that is spooky. Desire implies absence, a gap. My own feeling of anger indicated to me danger, danger to me in my role as Other, as guardian of the structure of the group, and, consequently, danger to the functioning of the group, to the symbolic dialogue. I was momentarily taken by my ego, by my imaginary. I became temporarily a member of the group and the place of the Other, my place as therapist was momentarily vacant. I did recover, though, and was able to return to the guardian of desire in the group and was able to not act out my anger.

I made a fairly simple comment that was helpful to the group. I said that it seemed to me that the leash that Matilde was talking about

48   THE DIALOGUES IN AND OF THE GROUP

could be the group. That she had come to the group to feel secure. That perhaps there was something that she was holding on to that was scary, and that now we were holding it for her. I added that the word leash could mean different things to each group member and went on to tie this meaning to what each member had said one by one.

At this point, I did not know anything about Lacan. I had not even heard his name. My orientation was object relations. I must say, though, that I have always had a keen interest in language, especially for the ways in which words, so to speak, turn around.

What was the meaning of my comment from a Lacanian perspective? It was to return the word to its place of signification so that it could be reinvited to the venerable halls of language. Before that, the word "leash" was a spectre in the group. By making it a metaphor, I brought it back from the Real to the Imaginary and the Symbolic. In doing so, I restored the radical Otherness of language, serving the function of "name of the father". This intervention and what ensued in the group is an example of what I call the dialogue *of* the group.

Now, years later, as I think about this anxious episode in the group, and using a Lacanian lens, my own internal dialogue informs me of my new reading of the group. Let me conclude these comments, indulging, if I may say that, in a bit of *jouissance*, in a back-to-the-future Lacanian rendezvous with my group. And I did/will speak about my group in this way.

Matilde:

1. Yes, you have a leash, you have this group.
2. But you don't have it. It comes from the Other, from the symbolic order that I represent not as an agent but as a function, as the one that holds this role representing the name of the father, the law of language.
3. We are holding you so that you can exist with us and not just ex-sist outside our community
4. Something has dropped off from your discourse, and we are holding on to it. It doesn't feel to us pet-like, but it does to you. We don't know what this something is, it doesn't have a name, even though you are using one. And because it doesn't have a name, it feels more like a spectre.
5. It is because we hold on to it that: (a) we are anxious, (b) you can continue talking.

6. One of our members is very angry because you have acted as a transgressor, and in doing so he feels endangered, and fears my death and his collapse into the unbearable *jouissance* that traumatised him as a child when his godmother would invite him to sleep with her while her husband was gone, and when, later on, he was raped.

7. Yet, I can also feel a respect and admiration for you because, by interrupting our discourse, you have forced us to confront in some way all of those spectres in the closet hidden behind the wall of language. You have penetrated the wall of language. At this moment we, like a hinge, operate between *jouissance* and desire. We must hold them together and hold them apart.

8. By interrupting us you have begun for us a process of interpretation. It is the only way that we can go back from this frightening real to the more liveable imaginary and symbolic. You have become my potential ally.

9. The group is very anxious because this object of desire, this *objet petit a* that I, as a therapist, represent for the group and that through me each member of the group can become for each other, this *objet petit a* that must remain veiled has somehow appeared; because it is a lack, it comes only as a frightening spectre and what we anticipate through this apparition is death. The death of meaning. The flight of the signifier. The absence of the dialogue of the group.

10. Yet, again, by bringing us in contact with death, you make me think of my role as a Lacanian, very much like the number -0-. I am nothing, nada, zero, lack. And yet I am needed for you to count up and to count down. I am needed as zero for you to be able to count on each other. Or, again, I am occupying the place of a very important signifier, representing you, the ineffable subject, to another signifier.

As I have said before, other psychoanalysts, especially Winnicott, have influenced my thinking and my way of working in the group. Those that have done AGPA institutes with me in the past few years and the therapists that have worked with me in the Washington School of Psychiatry have often remarked that, although I seem very passionate about my Lacanian orientation, there is a clear influence of Winnicott in my style. They are right. Their comments reflect my two central orientations as I work with the group. So, let me add just a few comments inspired by this other great mentor of our profession.

50   THE DIALOGUES IN AND OF THE GROUP

Winnicott did not quite talk about desire with the breath and scope that Lacan did, but he, like a good poet, said many similar things in his own way. In *Playing and Reality* (1971), he writes,

> Freud did not have a place in his topography of the mind for the experience of things cultural. He gave new value to inner psychic reality, and from this came a new value for things that are actual and truly external. Freud used the word sublimation to point the way to a place where cultural experience is meaningful, but perhaps he did not get so far as to tell us where in the mind cultural experience is. (p. 95)

Well, Winnicott went on to try to develop this, and I believe that Lacan succeeded perhaps more than anybody else in this endeavour. Winnicott came close to the concept of desire with his concept of illusion and the concept of the transitional object. He continues,

> It is usual to refer to 'reality testing,' and to make a clear distinction between apperception and perception. I am here staking a claim for an intermediate state between a baby's inability and his growing ability to recognize and accept reality. I am therefore studying the substance of illusion, that which is allowed to the infant, and which in adult life is inherent in art and religion, and yet becomes the hallmark of madness when an adult puts too powerful a claim on the credulity of others, forcing them to acknowledge a sharing of illusion that is not their own. We can share a respect for illusory experience, and if we wish we may collect together and form a group on the basis of the similarity of our illusory experiences. This is a natural root of grouping among human beings. (ibid., p. 3)

Here, Winnicott is talking, on the one hand, about the reality of the symbolic that the child gradually acquires and, on the other hand, the area of phantasy, of something that is left over from the symbolic, something that refuses to fully enter the symbolic order. He says, poignantly, that this area of illusion is allowed to the infant, and that in adult life is central in art and religion and the foundation for the various groupings in society. At the same time, he says, when anybody puts too powerful a claim on these important illusions and tries to force them on to other people, requiring them to accept them as their own, it becomes the hallmark of madness. Witness the present struggles in our modern societies with various ideologies from the left and the right demanding a full loyalty to their way of seeing and understanding the world.

CHAPTER SIX

Revolution, evolution: change and desire*

Part one: vicissitudes of the imaginary in the group

I went for a routine haircut in the suburb where I live. As the haircut proceeded, I began to feel drowsy. When my haircut was finished, I turned to my barber, a short, unassuming young lady, I said to her, "I was so relaxed, I was beginning to fall asleep." To which she responded, very matter-of-factly, "Well, you like to be touched."

Her words came upon me as if some curtain had been lifted from my eyes. I experienced something familiar to me, some simple truth that has since elaborated gradually in my mind, the product, I think, of my past work in analysis. Furthermore, I had a very pleasant feeling. Here was this young woman, very similar in attitude and simplicity to my sisters and the country people I originate from, giving me a message that she could not know then told me a lot about myself. In a sense, I was getting the benefit of a bit of analysis from somebody who, using the curtain of words, of signifiers, as Lacan puts it, removed the blinds to a room of my interior that had been nicely protected by my drowsiness.

---

*Much of this chapter contains revised material from a paper published in 2001 as: Chaos and desire: the simple truth of the unconscious in the psychoanalytic group. *Group Analysis*, 34(3): 349–363.

52 THE DIALOGUES IN AND OF THE GROUP

Here was an aspect of my unconscious drawn out cleverly by a matter-of-fact interpretation. The lady barber heard my words and responded. Her message surprised me for a moment, but led me to the reading of a familiar inscription that she pointed out to me unobtrusively. Something landed in my mind with the weight of a simple truth: "you like to be touched".

A barbershop is a group room, a place where stories are told and heard. Comments are made that can be at the same time totally frivolous, or inspiring, soothing, or boring. It is a room where several people come for a similar purpose, yet, each one likes to have their hair done in a special way; a place where each person talks as if he is alone with the barber, yet the room is usually filled with the presence of other customers. A barbershop acts as a group container for individual dialogues that the barber learns to hear as the uninterrupted monologues of his customers. Perhaps, the barbershop is akin to the psychoanalytic group.

Let me move away from this barbershop to my group room where I practise psychoanalytic group psychotherapy. Most of the time, in this room, I am the designated "barber". But the reality is that in the psychoanalytic group each member is potentially a barber and a customer. I will present to you a situation from a group in transition and will attempt to explore some aspects of the work with the unconscious in the psychoanalytic group.

Contextual background

At the time, I had been conducting two therapy groups. The number of patients had come down to five in one group and four in the other. I began to consider inviting these two groups to join in one new group. I had several ideas in mind: to have a better mix of men and women, to facilitate the work with a variety of issues with a richer dynamic in the new group, and to test the patients' disposition and my own to undertake this change, which could prove beneficial but also present some difficulties.

Perhaps each one of these groups was like a barbershop that had lost clientele and the richness of the stories, complaints, and tales of woe of the Imaginary dialogues could not be heard. Instead, perhaps, the spectre of the Real was around the corner, the intensity of very small groups not ready yet to move into uncharted territory.

After some personal struggle as to the pros and cons, I presented my decision to each group and gave them two months to work on the thoughts and feelings related to this change.

One group, Group A, had two women, Arcadia and Julia, and three men, Rodrigo, Alvaro, and Stanford. The other group, Group B, had one man, Jonathan, and three women, Adelle, Belinda, and Ortensia. Let me call Group A the optimistic group, and Group B the mixed group.

GROUP A	GROUP B
Arcadia, Alvaro, Julia, Rodrigo, Stanford	Adelle, Belinda, Ortensia, Jonathan

A central figure in Group A was Arcadia. This was her second round of group therapy. In the past, her common reaction to any new person entering her group was very negative. In this case, when I announced the possible merger of the two groups into one, she said that she was surprised by her own reaction. She now looked forward to the merger and felt this would add new life to the group. The other members, Julia, Rodrigo, Alvaro, and Stanford fell somewhere between looking forward to it and a wait-and-see attitude.

In Group B, Adelle was also a central character. She responded very negatively to the idea and said that she most probably would leave the group. Among many of the reasons that she gave, one had to do with Stanford, a member of Group A.

Adelle's group knew of Stanford. He had been in her group for a brief period of time and had then withdrawn one year before. In making the announcement of the merger, I told Adelle's group that Stanford had come back into therapy and was now a member of Group A. I also told Stanford that he would re-encounter some of the members from his previous group. I felt that this was information that both groups needed to have.

Stanford, in his previous group, had become for Adelle a central representation for her negative reactions to men. He was a young man in his mid-twenties, about half Adelle's age. He appeared often as withdrawn, angry, and tense. She felt that she had enough difficulty dealing with men close to her age and that Stanford was way beyond her reach, somebody to whom she could not relate. She could not see herself opening up with him in the group. She remembered an interaction with him before his withdrawal from the group where he had expressed strong negative comments to her.

Adelle had been in group psychotherapy previously, with another therapist, and felt that she had benefited a great deal from it. She was then in individual therapy with another therapist, but came to a point of feeling stuck and not being able to move forward. She had stopped that therapy and come to me for group and individual therapy. She had been now in this combined treatment for two years. Adelle's basic complaints related to intense feelings of loneliness, doubts about being able to find a man and be married. She had had a number of men in her life, but had not been able to meet the one that she could marry. Adelle's basic comment on the group merger was: "I am not going to change anyway, so it is useless for me to start all over again with a new group." She repeated this theme in a variety of ways during the sessions prior to the merger.

The new group

The first session of the new group was eventful. Rodrigo, who had been absent for five weeks because of job-related travel, was rather abrupt in reacting to a story by Julia about her new church. He used a four-letter word to describe those who go to church. Julia was upset at Rodrigo's flippant comment. Arcadia joined in, and Alvaro felt that Rodrigo was going back to old behaviour. So, essentially, all of the members of Group A (my "optimistic group"), had a very mixed response to Rodrigo's opening salvo coming from within their own ranks. However, Alvaro was quick to point out to the now sub-group B members that Rodrigo was actually a very soft and warm man, very intelligent and highly cultivated.

In sub-group B, Belinda was missing because of surgery. Adelle went on to list her reasons for not staying in the group. Ortensia was quiet, but obviously struck by what was going on in the group and concerned about Adelle's continuing threats of leaving. She did not want her to leave the group. She strongly identified with some of her complaints. As for Jonathan, he became almost immobilised by Rodrigo's salvo. He said he did not know what to say, he could not find words. He added, though, that he found his own reaction to

Rodrigo's comment quite remarkable. In this first session, sub-group A appeared for a moment rather chaotic and sub-group B was in shock and with a passive stance toward the newcomers.

These initial reactions point out already to a movement of initial disturbance in both sub-groups. The realm of the Imaginary, of the dialogues *in* the group, has been rattled and cohesiveness is not present, but anxiety is on the rise and acting out appears as a coping solution. We could say that there is a tension between the *ideal ego* of the group (idealised identifications) and the *ego ideal* (the symbolic structures of the superego). In Lacanian terms, it is a tension between the Imaginary and the Symbolic. In my own terms, it is a moment where I and the group are caught between the dialogues *in* the group, the prime subject matter needed for exploration at this time, and the dialogues *of* the group, the possibility of bringing out the Symbolic repressed and being acted out in the Imaginary dialogues

One month later

In this session, Belinda is still missing because of surgery. Julia announces that she is deciding to change careers and move from a highly technical and well-paid computer manager's role to become a high school teacher. I ask Stanford about his thoughts on Rodrigo's comments and he basically growls at me and tells me that he has no thoughts. To this, Rodrigo comments, "Well, the way you answered, it is not as if you have no thoughts." Stanford feels empowered by this comment and goes on to tell the group that he was run off the road by a drunken driver the night before. He had to walk for a mile and a half.

Therapist (Th):	Are you glad you are alive?
Stanford (S):	Yes.
Th.:	Some time ago you would not have felt that way.
S:	I think you are right.

This leads to a dialogue between Rodrigo and Stanford. Rodrigo talks about a recent skiing trip with his wife. During the trip, he had many thoughts about disaster and dying, and his wife dying. Jonathan becomes interested, and says to him, "I don't understand." Rodrigo is somewhat irritated and says, "I thought it was obvious what I was saying." Adelle addresses Rodrigo and questions him about his reluctance to explain. Rodrigo is clearly cautious and negative about Adelle's remark. Rodrigo says that he feels safe within the group, but outside the group he feels endangered. He tells me that he is very upset with me because I mailed his bill to his office address rather than his home address. "That's your sloppy work," he says. "I have given you my address many times."

In the meantime, for the past two sessions, Arcadia's initial optimism over the group merger has changed dramatically. She has felt caught between the disapproval of one of her "allies" in her group, Julia, and is very upset with other members of sub-group B, especially Jonathan, whom she feels is pre-judging her. In some way, I feel that she is falling between the cracks during this merger. She announces that she is going to leave the group at the end of the month (this is the first session of the month). She arrived half an hour late at this session, and brought some knitting. This has been symptomatic of her behaviour in the past when she is bored or anxious. I ask her, "How are you feeling, what is happening?"

She tells the group that she went home from work before coming to the group. She worried that she had left the oven on and worried about her cat. The group had talked about her being so angry the session before. As time goes on, I say to her, "Your concern about the oven being on might have something to do with the heat in this group the last session." She quickly responds, "No, I don't think so. You always put more into my thoughts than what they mean. I don't feel comfortable. I feel that I am starting all over again and all the progress that I had made is evaporating. Coming here tonight I felt that terrible anxiety that I used to feel, like panic. I had not felt that in a long time."

I ask Ortensia, the quiet one, "What are your thoughts? Don't think too hard." She responds, "Well, I make a distinction between safety and comfort. I don't think I will gauge my staying or leaving the group on the basis of comfort. But I know I need safety to be able to talk about my anxiety, my discomforts."

Rodrigo fires another salvo and tells Arcadia (they are fond of each other) that she should have kicked Jonathan. Adelle's attitude has begun to change noticeably and she talks with enthusiasm about a recent workshop she organised in a nearby city (she is a very educated woman and quite competent in her line of work). She talks about her pleasure in speaking Spanish with two other colleagues from Latin America. Alvaro talks about an imminent interview for a new job and about a wonderful secret. His secret is about his own little group, his marital therapy with another analyst and me. We meet weekly, the four of us, and he feels that his relationship with his wife is improving dramatically and gives some examples. Julia asks Jonathan about his interview for a new job. Rodrigo and Jonathan continue to interact with each other and I can tell that Jonathan, although still cautious with Rodrigo, is warming to him, finding him a very interesting character and becoming more and more curious about his own reactions to him.

Rodrigo brings two dreams. In one, he is smoking a cigarette and somebody else is also smoking with him. He knows that when the cigarette ends he is going to die. Yet, he seems relieved rather than anxious. In another dream, I am in the dream, filling out a form in triplicate, one is green, another yellow, and the third one white or neutral in colour. His wife gets one, indicating that somehow she has finished her therapy and she is all right. He then cannot find his form, or the one intended for him. The whole group joins in associations to Rodrigo's dreams, pointing out, among other things, that since he is not a smoker, the images seem to relate to something happening in the group.

After listening for some time to various comments, I make the following interpretation to Rodrigo: "You have to let a penis die before you can have your actual penis. And if that can happen, even though it is a death, it is also a relief." Rodrigo thinks for a moment and then says, "I don't know exactly how, but it sounds right. I just think that what you are saying sounds right."

Perhaps this is a moment of a simple truth. The group has helped me say something to a group member that appears to him quietly convincing.

PART II

CHAPTER SEVEN

Revolution, evolution: change and desire*

Part two: from identification to the desire of the other

The particular group situation that I have presented before can illuminate some aspects of the work with the unconscious in the psychoanalytic group. I will point out, first of all, that the changes in these groups amounted to a modification of some parameters of the analytic frame while others remained constant. Those aspects that changed were: the day of the meetings for the new group, and the membership of the new group, with all of its dynamic implications. Some of these were: expanded possibilities for role identification and differentiation, greater stress on competitive aspects for each member and greater anxiety over issues of cohesiveness of the self, affect and behaviour regulation, basic trust, belonging, identity, and capacity to maintain the therapeutic culture in the new group. Those aspects remaining constant were: the same therapist, the same amount of time, the same fee, and the same therapeutic method of exploration.

It is important to stress here that, in the new therapeutic situation, once the two groups have come together to form a new group, the

---

*Some of this chapter features revised material from a paper published in 2001 as: Chaos and desire: the simple truth of the unconscious in the psychoanalytic group. *Group Analysis*, 34(3): 349–363.

62   THE DIALOGUES IN AND OF THE GROUP

new therapist and group members become a new group. For each member, the therapist has changed. The vertical transference and the horizontal transference have been disturbed, and they must be elaborated carefully for the group to survive, and for each member to continue the therapeutic work.

Each member experienced a variety of reactions that could be summarised as follows: those from Group A (the "optimistic group") manifested as a whole a greater degree of activity and aggression within themselves and toward Group B. Those from Group B were, at the beginning, more passive and even somewhat shocked and paralysed, but gradually began to establish a place for themselves that, at times, was remarkably different from their previous one before the group merger.

I will point out some individual manifestations of the transference. From Group A: Arcadia, who originally is looking forward to the new group, becomes increasingly anxious, mistrustful, and disappointed. She asks to go back into individual therapy with me and, as announced, she leaves the group at the end of the month. She does stay for four sessions after her announcement, and is able to experience some degree of challenge and respect from the group members.

Julia continues flourishing, working with major life issues after divorce: change of name, selling her home and moving to an apartment, changing careers, and continuing exploration with changes in her sexual identity. She begins to consider leaving the group. Rodrigo also begins to talk about leaving the group in a way that he has not been able to approach before in his therapy. At this point, he has done what he considers a quite productive eight-year analysis with another analyst, and I have worked with him and his wife in marital psychotherapy for several years. He considers the marital therapy also fairly significant in positive changes for himself, yet, after that therapy, he has stayed in group therapy with me for three years. In the first of his two dreams, I might be the one smoking a cigarette along with him. The dream about the form in triplicate (we were a form in triplicate: his wife, green?, he, yellow?, I, white?) might represent his still unresolved struggle to leave me, whereas his wife did. As the initiator of salvos in the new group, this might have to do with a movement toward the giving up of taking my place with the mother group, but not without some final attempts at "smoking with the therapist". The impending death, at the end of the smoke, signals perhaps the relief of not having to be the chosen phallus, and the recognition of a basic lack that can free him.

Alvaro begins to talk more openly about "his secret", his special relationship with another analyst and with me in the marital psychotherapy. He begins to talk about having fun in therapy. At the same time, however, in one of the following weeks he forgets about his marital session, and the week after, he forgets the group session. This is totally new, Alvaro never forgets about his sessions. Is this new behaviour in Alvaro a manifestation of what he calls "fun", meaning a capacity to be ordinary, to also forget, and not to have to be the assistant to the therapist, reminding the other members of the group about attendance, being the substitute father, as he had to be in his family of origin?

Stanford, the youngest member from Group A, begins to get more involved with the old and new members and seems to begin to break out of his isolation. At the same time, though, he experiences great confusion and requests individual sessions in addition to the group.

As for the members of Group B, Jonathan and Adelle move into a new gear. Jonathan, after his initial shock, begins to have quite graphic incestuous dreams and his capacity for exploration seems to begin to rival that of Rodrigo. Adelle, who appeared determined to leave the group, becomes invigorated and her depression begins to change dramatically. She declares that she likes the new group and becomes freer in the exploration of her feelings and thoughts. Ortensia, although still remaining fairly quiet, opens up more and seems to begin to come out of her shell. Belinda, however, absent for a number of sessions because of her surgery, becomes disorientated, confused, and, for quite a few sessions, cannot move off a fairly concrete stance in the way she hears group comments.

Addressing the unconscious in the new group

The stirred-up landscape in this new group requires that I look at both intrapsychic aspects and cultural phenomena. I find some of Lacan's methods of talking about the unconscious quite useful in understanding the communications in this new group. Let us review once more some theoretical questions and applications to my work with this group.

64   THE DIALOGUES IN AND OF THE GROUP

For Lacan, "the unconscious is structured like a language". This means that the unconscious is a discourse, and it is a discourse that speaks to us. It speaks to us through the linguistic forms of metaphor and metonymy, in the same ways that the dream, according to Freud, speaks to us through condensation and displacement.

This discourse that speaks to us comes from the position of an Other. This position Lacan calls "transindividual". The unconscious surprises us. It manifests a basic *spaltung* (splitting), a profound division of the subject. Furthermore, this otherness relates to the primary Other, the mother, and later on to language, to the symbolic Other, to the law of the father, through which the child enters into the Oedipal, triangular relations. The child's imaginary relationship begins to change as language develops. Lacan discusses at length Freud's child observation of his nephew and the beginning words of the child *Fort . . . Da* as a key example of the function of language, and of the constitution of the subject.

This step into the Symbolic, at the same time as it begins to free the child from the Imaginary, alienates him/her through the wall of language and leaves a permanent mark in the human being as a divided subject, as always experiencing a lack-in-being that propels his/her desire. This constitutes two basic steps of alienation. The first one is the alienation into the ego, into the imaginary. The second one is the alienation into language, into the symbolic. Because it is through language that each one of us receives the desires of the Other (first of all, mother, then other family members, and the specific and general culture), the attention to the symbolic is crucial in bringing the human subject to confront his/her desire.

The recognition by the subject of his/her desire, and the naming of it, is central to Lacan's view of the function of analysis.

> That the subject should come to recognize and to name his desire, that is the efficacious action of analysis. But it isn't a question of recognizing something which would be already given, ready to be coapted . . .
> In naming it, the subject creates, brings forth a new presence in the world. (Lacan, 1954–1955, pp. 228–229)

How did the unconscious desires of the members of this group come out? I will point out the following dynamics as indicators of the movement from temporary "chaos" to "desire" in the merging of the groups:

1. Personally, as a clinician, I had to examine several aspects of my motivation in stimulating this change, and of the dangers and potential benefits for the therapeutic work.

2. As the change got under way, seesaw movements from faith to scepticism, interest and indifference, acceptance *vs.* rejection, engagement *vs.* fleeing, love and hate, omnipotence and impotence, life and death, all became apparent in the discourse of the group, sometimes brought about by dreams or by the acting out of some members. Some of the typical individual ego states were re-enacted in the central transferences to the therapist and the group as a whole, and in the multiple transferences from member to member.

3. The positions that individual members and each group took before the announcement of the merger began to shift, in some cases to exactly the opposite of the previously held convictions and attitudes.

4. Members began to find in the newcomers missing but repressed good qualities about themselves. They also, though, rejected, denied, and repressed bad aspects that related to them.

The partial change in the frame of these two groups, as they became a new group, brought up powerful repressed aspects of the unconscious. There was a heightened degree of anxiety. Aspects of resistance, repetition, and acting out were clearly present during the sessions and the basic psychoanalytic stance was put to the test.

Winnicott has written with eloquence in reference to the importance of the holding environment: "for the neurotic, the couch and warmth and comfort can be symbolical of the mother's love; for the psychotic it would be more true to say that these things are the analyst's physical expression of love" (1975, p. 199). In these groups, the one member I was more concerned about with regard to possible decompensation was Stanford. I agreed to see him individually in addition to the group.

An ongoing, long-term group develops aspects of what we may call an institution; by bringing the two groups together, I introduced a significant factor of change to the institutional container. This aspect of institution is not unrelated to the real, to something that resists

66   THE DIALOGUES IN AND OF THE GROUP

symbolisation. We can say, then, that the work with this new group rattled the institutional aspects of the previous groups in such a way that the experience of the real became more apparent in the new group and put a greater demand on the work with the imaginary (*in*) and symbolic (*of*) aspects of the transference. I find it useful here to bring the comments from the Argentinean analyst, Jose Bleger (1967) on the analytic relationship as an institution, and on the implications for the work of the unconscious when the basic frame (institution) is disturbed. Although he is not a Lacanian, I can certainly see how his thoughts are applicable. He suggests that,

> A relationship which lasts for years, in which a set of norms and attitudes is kept up, is nothing less than a true definition of institution. The frame is then an institution within whose bounds certain phenomena take place, which we call behavior . . . each institution is a portion of the individual's personality; and it is of such importance that identity is always, wholly or partially, institutional in the sense that at least one part of the identity always shapes itself by belonging to a group, institution, ideology, party, etc. (1981, p. 460)

Bleger goes on to demonstrate that this organised or stable frame becomes the repository of the psychotic, symbiotic, or non-differentiated part of the self that he also calls the non-ego or meta-ego. He adds that

> . . . the frame is a permanent presence, like the parents for the child. Without them, there is no development of the ego, but to keep the frame beyond necessity, or to avoid any change in the relationship with the frame or with the parents, there may be even a paralysis of development. (ibid., p. 464)

These comments point to the importance of the holding environment, yet, at the same time, to the need for a measure of anxiety to do the psychoanalytic work. The group needs the holding environment to experience the safety necessary, as Ortensia expresses it well in one session. On the other hand, if anxiety is absent, the work with desire becomes thwarted.

Pointers to desire in the new group

Some key phrases and attitudes orientated me to the dialogue of the group in the new format. These are some examples: first, the group members utterances and then, in italics, my internal wonderings, listening for the *desire* hidden in these comments:

"I am not going to change anyway."

Unless the Other opens the possibility for my desire.

Rodrigo's salvos in the first session of the new group and Alvaro's defence of Rodrigo to the group.

What is my place in the new group vis-à-vis my therapist, my fellow group members, my wife?

"I don't know what to say, I don't have words. . . . I am so struck by my reaction, why am I so paralysed by Rodrigo's comments?"

Suddenly I experience a part of me that I cannot put words to but feels like a part of me. . . . As I continue in my wonderings about Jonathan, a fairly obsessive character, my thoughts are that he has been thrown off from the place of the Cartesian subject, of the cogito, of the "I think, therefore I am" to the Lacanian subject of the unconscious, I don't know, I doubt, I don't have certainty, therefore I can be there where I am spoken.

Stanford growling at me and his utterance, "I have no thoughts."

I cannot think rationally at this moment. I am growling at you to wake you up to my underlying terror. In this space I cannot desire.

"Are you glad you are alive?" (therapist to Stanford).

You have come to this group because you can be alive here in the holding environment of this group even if what you can do right now is only growl.

"That's your sloppy work, I have given you my home address many times."

I am freer to confront you now in the new group, I don't have to idealise you as much.

"You always put more into my thoughts than what they mean."

I am not ready to deal with the symbolic in this new group. You and Jonathan are trying to analyse me before you know me. Get off.

"Well, I make a distinction between safety and comfort."

THE DIALOGUES IN AND OF THE GROUP

I need to hold for me and for the group the two sides of myself, the anxious one and the safe one. I think that the desire of my therapist and the group is for me to be a bridge now in the group. If I want to stay I must help others. What do I want?

Stanford's and Rodrigo's theme of death and subsequent comments by the group on his dreams.

Maybe we can help each other find out our desire since both of us have faced events in our lives close to the experience of death of desire. We have been close to stopping being human subjects.

Adelle letting the group know about recent success and her pleasure at speaking Spanish.

I am beginning to experience a certain jouissance and I can acknowledge a new freedom to be angry rather than fear men in this new group. This makes me freer also to speak the same language as my therapist. What do I want from him?

All these phrases and actions that speak have made me realise in writing this article how little I knew while in the group of the power of my position and the position of the group for each member through this process. It is clearer, now, how much I was in the position of an Other for the group, and how powerful this transference was in the reawakening of conflicting desires in the group members. It is often only in retrospect that the dialogue *of* the group, the dialogue of the unconscious in the group, can be recognised, as opposed to the dialogue *in* the group, the dialogue of consciousness, the imaginary dialogue, that can be apprehended as it happens. The diachronic, the historical flow of the dialogue *in* the group hides the synchronic, the dialogue *of* the group.

Conclusion

The force of the repetition compulsion comes out in a number of the previous examples and points out the patients' attempts at maintaining endless possibilities at the expense of defining necessities. In other words, what the patient is trying to avoid through repetition is a simple truth. To point out the unconscious is to take a step that stops

REVOLUTION, EVOLUTION: CHANGE AND DESIRE PART TWO   69

contingency, to give way to what at times might appear as an "ordinary" realisation, one that, however, might have far-reaching effects for the person. Miller (1995), the editor of Lacan's writings and teachings, says it well:

> The patient develops what we could present as a sequence of words, let us call them signifiers, which appear to be infinite, potentially Infinite. There is always, in the narration of one's life, a strong character of contingency. You experience your life by telling or articulating aspects of it: it was like this, but it could have been like that. I was somebody, but I could have been somebody else. What we have in the end is contingency. That is the meaning in logic of the possible. It happened like this, but it could have happened like that . . . when we discover—when you glimpse necessity in analysis—it's frequently, I won't say always, a gratifying moment for the patient. Be it hard necessity or horrible necessity, it feels like a victory over the unconscious. (1995, p. 237)

When the patient can really "see" things as they are and move the curtains blinding the eyes, what might appear is a simple truth, ordinary and inevitable, yet quietly freeing in its necessity. Lacan spoke of this necessity as something that is always being written in one's life. Analysis, then, becomes a reading, a reading of certain constants that are there all the time but need to be named. This naming and this reading are at the service of evolution. The process is, in many respects, a quiet revolution, one that today's technological man might want to reject as too alien to this age's wish for an imaginary paradise of virtual reality.

Felman, explaining Lacan and his attempt to return us to the radical discovery of Freud, writes,

> This is what constitutes the radical of the Freudian unconscious, which is not simply opposed to consciousness—but speaks from within the speech of consciousness, which it subverts. The unconscious is thenceforth no longer—as it has traditionally been conceived—the simple outside of the conscious, but rather a division, spaltung, cleft with consciousness itself; the unconscious is no longer the difference between consciousness and the unconscious, but rather the inherent, irreducible difference between consciousness and itself. The unconscious, therefore, is the radical castration of the mastery of consciousness, which turns out to be forever incomplete, illusory, and self deceptive. (1987, p. 57)

70 THE DIALOGUES IN AND OF THE GROUP

To arrive at some simple truths time and time again is the aim in the psychoanalytic group. The dialogues *in* the group and the dialogues *of* the group constitute a privileged intersubjective space, a constant back and forth between the imaginary expressions of the ego and the manifestations of the symbolic Other.

This intersubjective space stops both the individual and the group from fully imagining that they are God, that they have infinite possibilities. Yet, it is in the reading of the basic split that informs our lack of being that the individual members and the group as a whole can also find the profound desires that run like underground rivers and make we humans God-like.

The Puerto Rican poet, Julia de Burgos (1997), eloquently presents the dual dialogue going on in her own self. In the richness of her poetry, she speaks of the same basic concept that Lacan presents when speaking of the human subject. From her poem, "To Julia de Burgos", we can hear the human paradox.

Ya las gentes murmuran que yo soy tu enemiga porque dicen que en verso doy al mundo tu yo. Mienten Julia de Burgos, mienten Julia de Burgos. La que se alza en mis versos no es tu voz: es mi voz. Porque tu eres un ropaje y la esencia soy yo; Y el mas profundo abismo se tiende entre los dos.

[Already the people murmur that I am your enemy. Because they say that in verse I give the world your me. They lie, Julia de Burgos, they lie Julia de Burgos. Who rises in my verses is not your voice: it is my voice. Because you are the dressing and the essence is me; And the most profound abyss is spread between us. (pp. 2–3, translation by Jack Aguera)]

CHAPTER EIGHT

On knowing too much

I n this couples' group session, the therapists are working with the group members by listening to their utterances (what is said) and questioning the saying (the enunciation). As the session progresses, it is becoming clear that for one member of the group, Andrew, who is suffering from trauma, the ability to use the symbolic is presently reduced. The work in the group is overwhelming him with aspects from the imaginary and the real. For Gina, his wife, on the other hand, as difficult and intense as the sessions have been, she is able to use them; she can utilise the symbolic in a way that her husband is finding increasingly impossible.

The couple eventually leaves the group, and the therapists help them to do it in a way that maintains the psychoanalytic stance for both those leaving and those staying in the group. After leaving the group, Andrew and his wife continue their therapy as a couple. Yet, the time that they have spent in the group and the insights they have taken away from it are being used in a rather efficacious way by Gina. Here is a case where Gina is able to use the symbolic from the group with her husband. Andrew is able to listen to her as opposed to the group. The balance of the three registers is protected for the group and for the couple.

72   THE DIALOGUES IN AND OF THE GROUP

A couples' group session

Members: Chris and Carla (in their mid thirties)
Robert and Mitra (in their late twenties)
Leonard and Sandra (in their mid fifties)
Andrew and Gina (in their mid forties)
Jonathan and Marie (in their mid thirties)

Therapists: Marc and Aurelia (in their sixties and fifties, respectively)

The session is the first of a New Year. The group has had three weeks of interruption for the holidays.

Chris: Happy New Year (addressing Marc)

Marc: Happy New Year to you and everybody.

Marie: Anybody missing?

Leonard: Sandra called me fifteen minutes ago. She is stuck in traffic outside Dallas, Texas.

Marie: What about Mitra and Robert?

Marc: I am expecting them

(Robert arrives by himself, a few minutes late.)

Marc: Some new beards here in the group tonight

Robert: Yes, and I thought for a while that it had to do with my bad attitude at work, but you had wondered if it had to do also with my new assertiveness. I think it is the latter. [Makes reference to Leonard's ponytail.]

Mitra: [Arrives 10 minutes late and puts a bag by the right side of Marc almost behind his chair. Then goes and sits in the empty chair on Marc's left. Marc does not seem to notice the bag.]

Aurelia: [addressing Leonard]. Does Sandra have a mission? Coming all the way from Texas? What is she bringing?

Leonard: My mother's china, and a few other things and my rifle, which I never wanted to ship here and somehow my mother had not wanted to get rid of it.

Jonathan: Is that rifle of any significance to you?

ON KNOWING TOO MUCH   73

Leonard: None, it has none. I used it for target shooting when I was in high school but now it does not have any meaning. Nothing.

Aurelia: Nothing can be a lot of meaning

Gina: What do you mean? Sometimes nothing can mean nothing. Like the other day the lady who cleans my house broke a glass. She was concerned and I told her, "Don't bother, that does not mean anything to me." And a week later I broke a glass myself.

Marc: Gina, you seem curious about Aurelia's comment. Do you think there have been times when you have known a lot, or too much, and that has put you in a difficult place?

Andrew: Well, I prefer the façade of not knowing something. When my father got depressed, he wanted to tell me about things with my mother, and I said, no. I don't want to know. Keep it to yourself. I prefer to keep what I saw, whether it was true or false. I saw them as very happy. Now my mother had died and I did not want to know anything different about them, whether it was good or bad.

Marc: So, Leonard, you still think that rifle doesn't mean anything.

Leonard: Well, the only reason I would have wanted to have that rifle before would have been to show my daughter the proper use of it. My daughter has this boy friend who is into shooting and took her to a shooting range and showed her how to shoot. Then he left the pistol under the driver's seat of the car. We were all driving around with that pistol under the driver's seat for more than a week and not knowing. None of us has a licence to carry a weapon. And here I was carrying a concealed weapon in my car. It is very dangerous.

Marc: Concealed weapons. What do you all think about concealed weapons here?

Mitra: For me, it is my tongue. I try not to use it as a weapon, but sometimes it is not as concealed.

Gina: For me might be different. More like when I put my younger sister in her place because I am her older sister. Or when I hold back my intimacy from Andrew. For him, I think it is different, his withdrawal, his anger.

Aurelia: Well, I think in some ways, we are all concealed weapons in here. I am remembering the last time that we met, Marie. I

74   THE DIALOGUES IN AND OF THE GROUP

thought the depression that you told us you had in your adolescence that sent you to the hospital, that was a powerful weapon. There was a lot of energy in it. It was very painful for you and you had not realised how powerful all of that was until then.

Marc: How is it going for Gina and Andrew? Do you feel you are integrating into the group? (They have been the last couple to arrive in the group.)

Gina: Well, It has been crazy these two months. So much happening. We are talking and talking a lot. So many things happen here in this group, and sometimes we think it is this or that, and then we meet with you, Marc, for our session with you and our perspective changes dramatically and we see something we had not seen. It has been exhausting, but it has been rewarding. And no sooner do we get an answer than another question opens up around the corner.

Chris: I think it takes quite a while to get integrated into the group. I know it took quite a bit for me.

Jonathan: Well, very often, getting into the group is just letting it happen. I find sometimes that when I let things happen and listen, it is when I get the most out of it.

Chris: For me that is only the first step. But then being able to put into words what I feel is happening to me and then translate it into action, that I find very difficult.

Leonard: For me it is being able to talk about my pain

Marc: Mitra, you seemed to be listening to Leonard.

Mitra: What do you mean? I was thinking about my father and how abusive he was, but in fact I was thinking very differently from Leonard. I don't associate with his pain about his parent's divorce. I feel relieved that my parents divorced.

Robert: You talk about it as if that is something they should have done from the beginning. I had never heard you say that about your parents' divorce. Does that make you justify or think that you should divorce?

Mitra: Well, I am not saying that. I am saying though that if that is an option, I feel freer to do it, that is true.

ON KNOWING TOO MUCH   75

Robert: That is really something. I had never heard you talking about feeling relieved about your parents' divorce.

Chris: Does everybody here think that their parents had a bad marriage?

Gina: My mother divorced and married again and divorced and married once more. She seems to have a good marriage now.

Andrew: [raises his hand] I think my parents had a good marriage from what I saw; I don't want to know if they had a bad marriage. What you, Aurelia, said to Gina earlier in the session stuck in my mind. When you told her that sometimes she might have known too much or a lot. I am so angry now because I really know too much after the deaths of so many people in my life. I would gladly change my situation for what it was before when I did not know that much, before those deaths. We invent reality and that is often better than reality itself. I have a ball of anger and don't know what to do with it.

Marie: I think that my parents had a good marriage but I never saw them express affection to each other. They constantly protected me from bad news, and this was bad, very unreal.

Marc: [to Marie] Is this one of the things you appreciate about Jonathan, that he does not hide conflict from you?

Marie: Very much so. I prefer to know things even if they are really bad.

Chris: My parents talked and talked about divorce and never did it. In the last five years of my mother's life when she was suffering from cancer, she was cared for so well by my father.

Carla: If your parents had divorced, he would have found or learnt something new but not her. I think she was incapable of a good relationship, she needed help but she wouldn't ask for it. [After this she leaves earlier because she says she has to pick up her daughter.]

Aurelia: [to Carla and the group] I think what you are doing now, the way you pick up and go is very powerful. We should get back to that in the next session.

Jonathan: [to Leonard] You know, I had not realised until today, but you are really still suffering from your parents' divorce, and I don't understand why. It is not fair. Why can't you enjoy who you

76   THE DIALOGUES IN AND OF THE GROUP

are? You got a PhD, you are well respected in your field, you say you are a very different father with your children, but I still see you in pain.

Leonard: [appears very quietly moved] Well, I am working on it.

Jonathan: I am also beginning to understand something about you [to Andrew]. Right now you really have a great deal of difficulty enjoying your life. You seem so taken by so many different deaths in your family. Right now you know something about death, but you don't seem to want to know about life

Marc and Aurelia: [At some point towards the end of the session the therapists made some of the following comments.]

[To Jonathan] Do you think that Leonard and Andrew have some kind of key for you, and you for them? The way you have heard their comments about pain and death seemed very special.

[To Leonard] You were the first and the only boy. And often you had to buffer the anger and abuse of your father towards your mother. You were also often the object of his tirades. Is it possible that in some way this position gave you a sense of power, but one that you could not allow yourself to enjoy, or own as part of yourself? Taking pride in that role could have made you disloyal to your father and overly invested in your mother. Do you think that perhaps an aspect of your pain is designed to mask those kinds of meanings?

This was a remarkable first session of a new year. One can certainly wonder about the questions that the group had about the relationship of their therapists. We can look at three phases of the group as the metonymic flow of the signifying stories entered the dialogue *in* the group. A first phase is around the word nothing as a powerful repressing signifier, which is picked up by Aurelia. We can hear the action of repression: It's like, let nothing be nothing . . . I prefer the façade . . . My cleaning lady broke a glass . . . and I broke one a week later . . . that's all there is, a broken glass. In a second phase, the group is led by the therapists and some group members, especially Jonathan, to connect with the Symbolic, with the dialogue *of* the group. Leonard moves from his nothing to the dangerous weapon he had been carrying around under the driver's seat unbeknown to him. Other group members begin to connect dangerous weapons with the hostile behaviours they use in their relationships and the problems and divorces of parents. A third phase can be centred on Andrew's trauma. He complains of the excess of knowledge he has now. In his words "he has a ball of anger" and does not know what to do with it.

The conclusion of the session by the therapists centres on two men, Leonard and Jonathan, both working in the technology industry with advanced degrees supporting their technical knowledge. Both have, to some degree, taken a position as auxiliary therapists, especially Jonathan. The therapists' words are designed to maintain attention to their symptoms and not support their hiding behind the therapist's role, but without diminishing their important contributions to each other.

In the immediate background, all the couples seemed taken by very important events in their families of origin. Andrew was in a very precarious emotional state. He had lost, through serious and acute illnesses, a mother, a wife, and a daughter in a relatively short time. His new wife, Gina, seemed remarkable in her ability to assess situations, to know a lot about what was going on, and to sacrifice herself to keep her husband going. Gina felt, though, that her role was becoming increasingly overwhelming for her. In fact, she had become an over-functioning woman, keeping together the roles of wife of a traumatised man, mother of a stepson and a new baby, and a competent professional. In light of this, what can her words mean: "A broken glass is a broken glass . . ."?

Mitra and Robert, and Chris and Carla were struggling with whether to save their marriages or separate and divorce. Children were involved in both marriages and this was a central question they were also exploring in case they decided to end their relationships.

Leonard and Sandra were anxious to have a more rewarding and engaging relationship, but they seemed to end in constant squabbles and bickering. They were both professionals and quite bright and accomplished individuals, but their love life was severely limited. Jonathan and Marie were starting a family. They came from two very different cultures, one Latin, one North American. They had come to the group more to learn about themselves and be with other couples. They were not experiencing serious conflicts, but they both came from families where their roles had been central, yet confusing and depriving. They were very open to the group process and were able to learn

78   THE DIALOGUES IN AND OF THE GROUP

from the other members. Eventually. the latent conflicts from two very different histories and cultures began to show in the group .

In this group, central questions are raised by these couples as they struggle in their relationships in different ways. Among them are the question of knowledge, knowing too much, concealed weapons; questions of being and meaning, pleasure and pain. This was a session where the therapists tried to focus on the central issues of the unconscious, and transference, as manifested in different ways by each member.

In the following chapter, we will use the material from this session to expand on Lacan's concepts of Being and Meaning, Drive and Desire, Subject and Other, *Jouissance*, the Cartesian Subject and the Freudian Subject. We will end with a focus on Alienation and Separation, two central concepts Lacan moved to from his original emphasis on Metaphor and Metonymy.

CHAPTER NINE

Between being and meaning: between drive and desire

In the group session presented in Chapter Eight, the members occupy different positions with respect to unconscious knowledge. Andrew and Gina's comments can help us understand the division between being and meaning. Andrew has gone through massive trauma. He does not find any meaning. Right now, he feels he is mostly existing. Because of his trauma, Andrew has a fragile hold on the imaginary and the symbolic that permitted him, before the family deaths, to be alienated into language like any neurotic subject. He is frightened by the regression that is taking place in the group and that he is beginning to find intolerable. He is fortunate, though, because his wife, Gina, has a better grasp on meaning, although Andrew feels despair.

This couple used to come together to the session, Andrew holding Gina's hand most of the time and always sitting next to her. Gina says that so much happens in this group. She knows as much as the therapist, Aurelia, points out to her. She has so much to elaborate, to process for herself and for Andrew. In this sense, one can hear her comment back to Aurelia, "What do you mean, sometimes nothing can mean nothing?" as a kind of complaint related to all the "too much" from her husband that she has to deal with, putting her in the

80   THE DIALOGUES IN AND OF THE GROUP

role of too much meaning and very little being for herself. She has to maintain for herself and for her husband, Andrew, the system of signifiers that create meaning. This role, to an excess, interferes with her libido, her *jouissance*. Yet, she says it has also been very rewarding. Listening to the other members and going home and talking and talking about what has been brought up in the group. And, she adds, no sooner do you get an answer when another question comes around the corner. While her husband is, to some extent, paralysed, unable to use signifiers to re-establish a process of "reality", she is moving from signifier to signifier, tying together a number of issues for herself and her husband. This is a couple where the tension between being and meaning, or the Real and the Symbolic, is clearly manifested by their comments in the group. The challenges facing this couple are taken up, to some degree, by the rest of the members and contribute to the opening up in the group.

This couple did not stay too long in the group. Andrew began to feel immersed in an impossible way in his feelings regarding other members that he could not contain. As an example, he felt extraordinary rage towards Mitra, and proved unable to deal with it. He began to tell Gina that the problem did not lie with him, it was the group members, and Gina initiated the process of termination from the group, which happened in a helpful way.

In Andrew's and Gina's last session, Mitra was not present. Everybody in the group knew that they would continue meeting with Marc for joint sessions. In the next session, Mitra asked Marc to tell Andrew that even though she was also very angry with him, she actually had a lot of affection for him, which included love. Mitra had found in Andrew a powerful identification with her own father. Here is an example of the force of the lateral imaginary transference as a detour from the vertical transference to the therapist (in this case Marc) interfering with the work with the symbolic. Mitra began to approach it once Andrew left; before that, it was hard to let her recognise her love for Andrew, representing her father, and the forbidden *jouissance* that remained unconscious.

Gina profited a great deal in an unsuspected way. A few weeks after leaving the group, Gina and Andrew went on a summer vacation. In the hotel, Andrew began to stay in the room and not join her and the children in the first few days, overtaken by his depression. Gina's experience from the group gave her the freedom to confront him. She actually told him that if he had come on vacation to feel sorry for himself and spoil her vacation and that of the children, he could go home and she would finish her vacation with her children. To her surprise, this shook up Andrew in a good way; he stopped his withdrawal and joined the family around the pool of the hotel and began to participate in some activities. Gina was able to come into herself, in the sense of stopping the unending need to "understand" Andrew. Andrew, on the other hand, must, on some level, have realised that it was because of his wife that he could continue to hold on to meaning. Losing her would mean psychic death.

Alienation and separation

In his later years, Lacan began to move from the concepts of metaphor and metonymy to two other very important concepts, alienation and separation (see Figures 5 and 6).

The child, before birth, is already taken by the Other, by the signifiers of the desire of the Other (mother, father, relatives, language). The child comes to occupy a place in the Other, a place that, in that sense, is not his/her own. It comes from the Other. The desire of the mOther is passed to the child through language. When the child starts using the symbols of that language that carry the desires of those around him/her, the child becomes, in Lacanian terms, a true subject, a subject of language. If this does not happen, if language misfires and the child cannot come into the paradigmatic and syntagmatic structure of language, as pointed out before, the child is in psychosis. The name of the father has not functioned, and the child is stuck in being, unable to enter the process of life that requires the ability to use metaphor and metonymy, to develop meaning. In this process, for the child to become a subject, she must become alienated into language. It is, we could say, a forced choice. As Soler writes, "alienation is destiny. No speaking subject can avoid alienation. It is a destiny tied to speech" (1995, p. 49). As pointed out again by Soler,

> The Other as the locus of language—the Other who speaks—precedes the subject and speaks about the subject before his birth. Thus the Other is the first cause of the subject. The subject is not a substance. The subject is an effect of the signifier. The subject is represented by a

82 THE DIALOGUES IN AND OF THE GROUP

> signifier, and before the appearance of the signifier, there is no subject. But the fact that there is no subject does not mean that there is nothing, because you can have a living being, but that living being becomes a subject only when the signifier represents him. (ibid., p. 43)

But when the child comes into language, when she is taken by the signifier, there is something that does not completely fall under the signifier.

In other words, if language, the signifier, gives birth to the subject, there is a remainder, the drives, *jouissance* that cannot be completely taken over by the signifier. This remainder is object (a). Lacan says, "it is in this living being, called to subjectivity, that the drive is essentially manifested" (1978, p. 203). This means that the subject is complemented by (1) the signifier, and (2) *jouissance*, the drives. Lacan then presents his formula for fantasy, what the human uses to recover his drives in spite of the prohibitions and demands from the symbolic order. This formula simply expresses the particular ways in which the subject relates to the object of desire: it is read as the subject in relation to object (a): S <> a.

If we look at the two figures, 5 and 6, in the place of signifier 1 (what is called a master or primary signifier), we now encounter object (a). It is Lacan's way of saying that, as the subject works through her alienation, she must confront her desire. And, since desire is how the subject tries to respond to the Other, trying to bypass the drives, her *jouissance*, the subject must now face the task of subjectifying her desire. The subject must confront a choice *vis-à-vis* the Other and *vis-à-vis* the drives. That the object (a) comes to occupy the place of S1, then, means that the subject has gone through separation. For the subject to go through separation means that the subject must face castration, the rock of castration. Simply put, the subject must realise that he/she has been held down by language, by the master signifiers that took him/her in service to the Other. The subject is now faced with a new choice, to become responsible for his/her particular way of enjoying the object, and the options available to him/her to live with the Other in the social bond. We could say that Andrew was at a loss as to how to bring back into his life a relationship to another, to an object of love after suffering massive loss of the signifying ways in which he had been connected to life. In analysis, the analysand must traverse the fundamental fantasy, the way in which his drives achieve a compromise in confronting the Other. Even though this kind of work cannot happen in group in the way that is supposed to happen in individual analysis, it is very useful for the group therapist to consider the journey that the patient is following in pursuit of the resolution of his symptoms. Some patients can go further than others. Here, in this group, Andrew was reaching an impasse. He needed a more supportive treatment at the time, before he could move on to explore and confront his loss of meaning. Yet, he, like other similar patients in group treatment, can often leave powerful lessons for those that have not had to confront severe trauma. This is one example of how the struggles of one patient often empower the insight of another.

Let us pursue a bit further some of these concepts, using the dialogue from the couples group. Trauma can affect somebody in the way that it affected Andrew. Gina was serving the function of staying with him in a relationship that held him, while she was also able to hold on to meaning and not succumb to a symbiotic demand from Andrew to eliminate meaning. Andrew was avoiding a complete breakdown by holding on to Gina. All the main signifiers of his imaginary and symbolic registers were tested by three deaths in his family. He had been an executive in an important company and had never confronted emotional issues as challenging as the present ones. His staying in the group was pushing him in the direction of psychosis, and, in a certain sense, he was right, when using projective identification, in saying that the problem was the group. It was very important that his wife and the therapists understood his fragility and that the couple was helped to exit the group in a helpful way. One can hear his painful struggle when he says, "I am so angry now, because I really know too much after the deaths of so many people in my life. I would gladly change my situation for what it was before when I did not know that much, before those deaths. We invent reality and that is often better than reality itself." This is a clear expression of how the collapse of the Other can plunge the patient into the real. Another member of the group had said similar things at another time, even though she herself was not facing a trauma as acute as Andrew's. Yet, her realisation of how much she had been constrained by the original signifiers of her life led her to exclaim in one group session: "My life has taken a life of its own and I am not in it."

These expressions can help us understand how much we all maintain a necessary alienation through language. Andrew is now in the

84   THE DIALOGUES IN AND OF THE GROUP

direction of the real, into being; he has a fragile hold on the imaginary and the symbolic. Andrew is right, we invent reality; reality is framed by the image and the word. Without that, we are into the Real, we stop being human subjects, we are outside meaning, in a "too much" that is only being, in the "knowledge of too much", of the real. And the paradox is that in this "too much knowing" we know very little, if anything. Meaning could collapse into being in a way that puts the human out of the social bond.

Between jouissance and the subject of speech

Let us review the concept of *jouissance*. The French word *jouissance* was used by Lacan in different connotations as he developed his theory. It means enjoyment, but, in French, it also has the implications of sexual pleasure. Evans, in his *Dictionary of Lacanian Psychoanalysis* (1996), points out that "in the seminars of 1953–1954 and 1954–1955 Lacan uses the term occasionally, usually in the context of the Hegelian dialectic of the Master and Slave. The slave is forced to work to provide objects for the master's enjoyment, or "Jouissance" (p. 91). In later writings, the term becomes more clearly associated with orgasm and sexual pleasures. But again, as stated by Evans later,

> Lacan develops his classic opposition between *jouissance* and pleasure, an opposition which alludes to the Hegelian/Kojevian distinction between *Genub* (enjoyment) and *Lust* (pleasure). . . . The pleasure principle functions as a limit to enjoyment; it is a law which commands the subject to 'enjoy as little as possible'. At the same time the subject constantly attempts to transgress the prohibitions imposed on his enjoyment, to go 'beyond the pleasure principle'. However, the result of transgressing the pleasure principle is not more pleasure, but pain, since there is only a certain amount of pleasure that the subject can bear. Beyond this limit, pleasure becomes pain, and this 'painful pleasure' is what Lacan calls *jouissance*; 'jouissance is suffering' . . . The term *jouissance* thus nicely expresses the paradoxical satisfaction that the subject derives from his symptom, or, to put it another way, the suffering that he derives from his own satisfaction. (ibid., p. 92).

In the group, as a contrast to Andrew in the dynamics of drive and desire, is Leonard's dynamic position. He is well taken care of by

BETWEEN BEING AND MEANING: BETWEEN DRIVE AND DESIRE   85

repression. He is quick and clear to tell Jonathan that that rifle means nothing. It has no meaning, none. We are dealing here with a nothing of a very different kind from the nothing of Andrew. The nothing of Leonard is not the nothing of the too much of being. The nothing of Leonard is the too much of the signifier, too much of the Other of language in an empty shell of being. It is the nothing of the obsessive that flees from his desire, because his desire exposes him to excessive pleasure, to *jouissance*. We are dealing with the nothing of the utterance, or the statement, with the emptiness of speech cut off from the object of desire by repression. Yet, this is the same Leonard who more freely associates the more he is questioned and who ends up talking about the concealed weapon under the driver's seat. He is able to utilise, to some degree, the dialogue of the group to begin to tie the nothing together with something very dangerous, a concealed weapon, an unconscious weapon. And the therapist uses this signifier to question the group on aspects of the unconscious. The therapists begin to question the group on the concealed weapons of the drive, the fear of confronting the *jouissance* that is concealed by the pain, and the different approaches to this *jouissance* in the group.

Mitra is relieved by the divorce of her parents. There was too much suffering (*jouissance*) in her family role. Leonard, on the other hand, is still imprisoned by his pain, which he attributes in part to the divorce of his parents. What the therapists begin to question him on is whether this is a pain hiding the *jouissance* of his special role in the family.

Between Descartes and Lacan: between two kinds of knowledge.

Some of the other members of the group, Gina, Chris, Marie, and Jonathan, and, to a lesser degree, Carla, were able to more clearly fulfil the role of the psychoanalytic patient. Who is the subject of analysis, the subject who comes asking for help? What does Lacan mean by subject? This is an important question that can clarify, perhaps, some of the differences, for instance, between self psychology, ego psychology, object relations, and the Freudian version of analysis as developed by Lacan.

Lacan adopted Hegel's thesis that Descartes inaugurated modernity, that he laid the foundations for the subject of science. Descartes's

86   THE DIALOGUES IN AND OF THE GROUP

famous dictum, *cogito ergo sum*: "I think, therefore I am", tells us that the subject of the *cogito* is the subject of thought. Furthermore, for Descartes, this is a subject of certainty. Because I think, I am certain about my existence.

Soler (1995) explains the similarities and differences between the Cartesian subject and the Freudian subject. The Cartesian subject, she argues, is certain about his or her existence as presence, but not about his or her essence or essential being.

The Cartesian subject, the subject of thought and certainty, is not the subject of truth. "My thoughts can be true or false—never mind; they can be hallucinations, dreams, mistakes—never mind; when I am thinking, I am" (ibid., p. 41). The patient who asks for psychotherapy is the patient of suffering. It is also the patient of doubt, who does not know why s/he is suffering. In this sense, the analysand is a very different subject from the Cartesian subject. It is not a subject of certainty. The Cartesian subject is a subject of mastery. The subject of the unconscious, the Freudian subject, is a subject as slave. It is a subject subverted by the system of signifiers. As submitted to the system of signifiers, the subject is an effect, an effect of the signifier. But because there is suffering, we know that there is something more than just the effect of the signifier. The symptoms lead us to another aspect of the subject, that aspect that does not completely surrender to the Other of language. So the subject is, on one hand, the subject of thought and, on the other hand, this subject is intimately connected to the living being, to the subject of the drives that responds to the demands of society and rebels. This rebellion is manifested by the symptom. The symptom is, for the neurotic, a compromise between the subject of *jouissance* and the subject of speech. The rebellion from the drives goes beyond the limits allowed by the pleasure principle and the signifiers from the Other, and the result is suffering. Andrew does not want to know. He cannot fathom how to become responsible when he feels that fate has hit him unfairly. It is a delicate situation for him, the therapists and the group. He needs the holding of the imaginary, the empathy of his wife, the group members, and the therapists before he is able to rejoin the exploration required by the symbolic.

As we have said before, Lacan moved gradually from metaphor and metonymy as two organisers of the language of the unconscious to his concepts of Alienation and Separation. Miller has developed these schemas (Figures 5 and 6) to explain them.

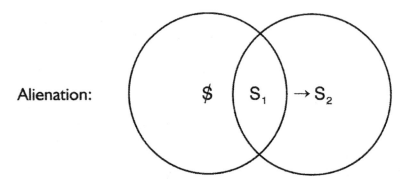

Figure 5. Lacan's concept of alienation.

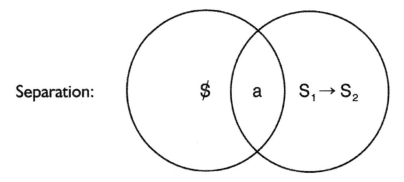

Figure 6. Lacan's concept of separation.

In alienation, the subject is taken by the Other, by language. He is a split subject (S) whose being is taken by signifiers. S1 is a master signifier. For instance, you are a bad girl, or a selfish man. These signifiers, if imprinted by the child from a context of certain demands of the Other, might determine how the child deals with relationships. If you are a bad girl, the way you love others will happen in reference to this master signifier. The desire of the subject is organised by the signifiers in the place of the Other.

In both alienation and separation, the subject is confronted with two lacks. In alienation it is the lack related to language. The signifier can never fully represent the subject, and, furthermore, the signifier starts in the Other and not in the subject. In separation, the being of the subject cannot be completely taken by the desire of the Other. There is a part of the subject's being that escapes the desire of the

88   THE DIALOGUES IN AND OF THE GROUP

Other. In Mitra, again, we can imagine that the divorce of her parents brings some relief, because the grip of her father's desire on her is lessened to some degree. She begins to question her own desire. In a sense, she might be more able to subjectify her desire, to be less at the mercy of the desire of the other.

In alienation, we are dealing with the identifications that have defined the person's emotional life. In separation, we are dealing not only with the identifications at the symbolic level, but with what the subject has been at a more substantial level in terms of his/her *jouissance*. At this level, the relationship of the subject to his fantasy (S <> a) is of central importance. By unravelling the subject's relationship to his fantasy, we find out the ways of *jouissance*, how the subject has tried to escape total alienation into the signifier.

I have used this particular session to illustrate some very dense and difficult concepts of Lacanian theory. I do not imagine they will be fully understood, in spite of the clinical examples that have been presented. What I hope I have made clear is that, for Lacan, as for Freud, the concept of the drive and the concept of the signifier, of the symbol, remain central in the understanding of the subject of the unconscious, which is the subject of analysis.

Perhaps the reader can appreciate now, using these Lacanian perspectives, the words of the popular song, "Is That All There Is?" We could hear them as the struggle between being and meaning, between *jouissance* and desire.

"Is That All There Is?"

> I remember when I was a very little girl, our house caught on fire.
> I'll never forget the look on my father's face as he gathered me up
> in his arms and raced through the burning building out to the
>   pavement.
> I stood there shivering in my pajamas and watched the whole world
>   go up in flames.
> And when it was all over I said to myself, "Is that all there is to a
> fire?"
>
> Is that all there is?
> Is that all there is?
> If that's all there is, my friends,
> Then let's keep dancing.

BETWEEN BEING AND MEANING: BETWEEN DRIVE AND DESIRE   89

Let's break out the booze
And have a ball if that's all there is.

And when I was 12 years old, my father took me to the circus,
    the greatest show on earth.
There were clowns and elephants and dancing bears
And a beautiful lady in pink tights flew high above our heads.
And as I sat there watching the marvelous spectacle, I had the
    feeling that something was missing.
I don't know what, but when it was over,
I said to myself, "Is that all there is to a circus?"

Is that all there is?
Is that all there is?
If that's all there is, my friends,
Then let's keep dancing.
Let's break out the booze
And have a ball
If that's all there is.

Then I fell in love with the most wonderful boy in the world.
We would take long walks by the river or just sit for hours gazing
    into each other's eyes.
We were so very much in love.
Then one day, he went away. And I thought I'd die, but I didn't.
And when I didn't, I said to myself, "Is that all there is to love?"

Is that all there is?
Is that all there is?
If that's all there is, my friends,
Then let's keep dancing.

I know what you must be saying to yourselves.
If that's the way she feels about it why doesn't she just end it all?
Oh, no. Not me. I'm in no hurry for that final disappointment.
For I know just as well as I'm standing here talking to you,
when that final moment comes and I'm breathing my last breath,
    I'll be saying to myself,

Is that all there is?
Is that all there is?
If that's all there is, my friends,

90   THE DIALOGUES IN AND OF THE GROUP

Then let's keep dancing.
Let's break out the booze
And have a ball
If that's all there is.
                    (Leiber & Stoller, 1968)

CHAPTER TEN

Conclusion

Between an answer and a question: personal musings on psychotherapy and spirituality

A t a meeting of the American Group Psychotherapy Association, I was a member of a panel of speakers coming from different cultural and religious backgrounds. We were asked to share our thoughts and our evolution as therapists as related to some form of spirituality. This is a modified version of my presentation. I submit this to the reader as a way to conclude. It is, of course, a moment where I share some of my subjectivity as informed by my professional life, and specifically by my study of Lacan.

I do not subscribe to every aspect of the Lacanian reformulation of Freud. This might have to do more with my limitations, due, in part, to a late arrival and insufficient training in his brand of psychoanalysis. I still find in my previous orientation, especially in object relations and self psychology, strong influences that accompany me in my practice. That being said, I have found in Lacan powerful incentives in my continued effort to understand and reach a bit closer to the human in me and in my patients. I will limit my musings to those aspects of Lacanian theory more related to my work as a psychotherapist and leave other more philosophical issues for another setting.

The word "spirituality" comes from the word spirit. The *Shorter*

92   THE DIALOGUES IN AND OF THE GROUP

Oxford English Dictionary, fifth edition (2002) gives, among others, these meanings:

> The animating or life-giving principle in humans and animals. The immaterial part of a corporeal being, especially considered as a moral agent; the soul. Mind, will and feelings. A mood or emotional state. The divine nature or essential power of God, regarded as a creative, animating, or inspiring influence, Holy Spirit. Evil spirits or demons. The general intent or true meaning of a statement as opposed to its strict verbal interpretation. (p. 2962)

The Cambridge International Dictionary of English (1995) emphasises two other meanings: (1) a particular way of thinking, feeling or behaving, especially a way that is typical of a particular group of people , an activity, a time, or a place. (2) The characteristics of a person that are considered as being separate from the body, and which many religions believe continue to exist after the body dies.

We can say that psychotherapy, and particularly group psychotherapy, addresses the mind, spirit, or soul of our patients. This mind or spirit that I am talking about, however, is an embodied mind, not the Cartesian mind. It is a spirit anchored in the human flesh and the body of culture and traditions of the groups and societies from which we all come, styled in unique human predispositions that include a particular orientation to the purpose of life. This orientation might or might not be infused by a faith in the divine, with all the corresponding accoutrements of a religious tradition.

In *Civilization and its Discontents*, Freud writes,

> The question, 'what is the purpose of human life?' has been asked times without number; it has never received a satisfactory answer; perhaps it does not admit of such an answer . . . One can hardly go wrong in concluding that the idea of a purpose in life stands and falls with the religious system. (Freud, 1930a, p. 74)

Freud decides not to enter this territory. He does say that it falls within the religious system. There is a contemporary current in our field that considers spirituality, rather than a specific religion, the place where this issue can be approached

I am stating that, as group psychotherapists, we attend to the embodied mind and take on a spiritual endeavour that requires

CONCLUSION   93

constant training, reflection, and dialogue with other related disciplines. As therapists, we enter into a personal engagement with what I would call an ethics of the soul that include the ethical principles and standards of our profession but that also go beyond that to a position of permanent creative tension with the accepted standards of our surrounding cultures. In this latter sense, our endeavour, although culturally informed, is also countercultural and revolutionary.

To bring some order to my wanderings, I will share with you three moments that speak to my trajectory as a therapist.

First moment

This brings me to the village where I come from in the Andes of South America. Many of my immediate relatives live within a three-block area of the hilly town. During one of my visits there, I was walking one day from the house of one of my brothers to the house of one of my sisters. Suddenly, on the sidewalk, a seven-year-old boy—one of my nephews—stopped me. "Uncle, where are you going in such a hurry?" he asked. I looked at this stocky and cute little boy, with open eyes looking at me waiting for the answer to some mysterious question he seemed to have in mind. Then I looked around on the main street of the village and saw everybody walking slowly, and going about the everyday business of life as if they were in no hurry to go anywhere; they just lived there. Then I understood my nephew's surprise. He saw me at that moment as an outsider. The pace of my walk put me in a very different rhythm from the rest of the town's people. And yet, I was his uncle, so what was wrong with me? I slowed down and we joined our pace, but I had been made aware of marching to the beat of a different drum. After being in the eastern USA for a long time, and having left my folks early in life, I truly did not fit there any more, even though I kept them in my mind and heart forever. I was now the member of another culture, another imaginary, and also part of a number of conventions and understandings of another language that separated me from my early beginnings. I felt calmer, became less anxious, and a bit more able to take in my surroundings. It was as if I had just landed in my body.

Psychotherapy as spirituality is a special language, one that, if we understand Freud's message, helps the human subject step out of the

94   THE DIALOGUES IN AND OF THE GROUP

ego into the other language of the unconscious. In a sense, it is a kind of fall, of landing into the human that has been hidden by culture. But the landing requires skill. To step out of one language into another takes time, dedication, and study. To use this kind of language to bring healing to the human being is a kind of discipline and art that never ceases to challenge the serious practitioner.

Second moment

Here I refer to my experience in Europe while studying and travelling there in 1965. I became greatly interested in the writings of Pierre Teilhard de Chardin, a scientist and Jesuit priest who began to run into trouble with Rome because of his *avant garde* thinking. I read some of his books, especially *The Phenomenon of Man* (1939–1940), *The Divine Milieu* (1926–1927), and a pamphlet published by the Vatican where he was questioned in detail on his ideas in conflict with the church's teachings.

I also took some time to visit a Protestant monastery in the little town of Taize, in France, where a Swiss monk, Brother Roger, was attracting hundreds of young people from all over Europe interested in some spirituality outside of the strict and old forms of their different upbringings. Just a few days in the company of these people, and listening to the simple message of its founder, opened my eyes to the common spiritual concerns of many contemporary Europeans coming from different religious orientations.

At the time, I also became acquainted by reading another book, by Roger Garaudy (1965), with a group of European intellectuals interested in the whole issue of faith apropos of the changes brought about by the ecumenical movement sparked by Pope John XXIII. This group was composed of Christians and non-Christians, believers and non-believers. For a period of time, they would get together and exchange their views on these issues.

The central message I took from one of the members of this group (I suppose a form of group psychotherapy) made a great impact on me: "What is the difference between you believers and those of us non-believers?" he asked. And then he himself answered, "For you believers God is an answer, for us on the other side, God is a question." These words encouraged me to discover another side of myself, one I had been scared of facing, the questioning part of me. The part of myself that wanted to be free to doubt, to be open to the unknown. I felt empowered by this message. I could have answers and questions. I began to follow my questions. In the process, longer rather than shorter, my answers have settled down a bit; others have disappeared; others remain in me as comfortable pillows upon which I still rest in the middle of my struggles. These influences, among others, led me to my eventual change of path, to a determination to become a psychologist, and specifically a psychotherapist.

Third moment

This begins with my discovery of Jacques Lacan in 1994.

Lacan set himself out to lead the return to Freud. He considered the new psychoanalytic theories of ego psychology and object relations as not fully representing Freud's thinking and his discovery of the unconscious. Lacan's writings have become for me a new opening, a question that helps me re-examine the answers I had arrived at from these other theories.

One way that I express the changes I have come to as I study Lacan is that theories such as object relations functioned for me as a mother theory. Lacan is more a father theory. I have welcomed this development in my thinking and I have been trying to apply Lacan's ideas in the Institutes I have been conducting at AGPA and other places around the country and internationally for the past few years. I can say that Lacan's basic concepts of the Real, the Imaginary, and the Symbolic, and how they inform the therapist's view of the human subject, frame for me key aspects of the ethics of psychotherapy

In applying his theory to my practice, I can say I am constantly working in a spiritual endeavour, held on one side by answers, challenged on the other side by probing questions. Some answers become questions and some questions lead to answers. Like growing trees, the answers require the winds to test and invigorate their foundation (vigour is one of the meanings of spirit). Some trees planted too shallowly do not make it. Others, with deeper roots, become more solid and grow healthy and strong. I can certainly relate to the comments of one of the women in the couples group presented before. "No sooner do you get an answer than a question comes around the corner."

96   THE DIALOGUES IN AND OF THE GROUP

Somebody might ask me at this point: "What do you see as the shortcomings of Lacan's approach, especially as it applies to the work with the group?"

No theory has all the answers. Other theories, such as object relations, self psychology, relational and interpersonal ones, emphasise the interconnectedness of all of us, and the central place of empathy in their theorising and in the clinic.

For me, this is related to what I call the dialogues *in* the group. I find it easier to get help for certain comments from these theories. Perhaps Lacan does not seem to contribute as much to this aspect in the clinic, in spite of the fact that the concept of desire is at the centre of his theory.

But, for me, his courageous stance on the subject's confrontation with her desire, with the fantasies in the weaving of her *jouissance*, and, more than anything else, with the subject's confrontation of her division between drives and the Other, between being and meaning, between the Real and the Symbolic, is worth pursuing in the group. It speaks to what I would want the group to become for each member as well through the dialogues *of* the group. A place where not only the imaginary dialogues come into the group with full vitality, but also one where the palpitations of the key signifiers of the person's history are recognised. A place for the dignity of each person's monologue, as revealed through the words that come into meaning. A place where the subject is situated between the conventions established by the Other and the unknown, not revealed or impossible to speak real.

To begin my conclusion to these wanderings, I will bring two examples, the first from my reading of Bertand Russell's autobiography and the Spanish philosopher Ortega y Gasset, and the second from the death of a member of one of my groups. In his self description, from *The Autobiography of Bertrand Russell* (1951), the English mathematician and philosopher relates an episode that takes place in early 1901. He and his wife were staying with Alfred N. Whitehead and his wife in Professor Maitland's house in Downing College.

Russell writes of coming back to the house and finding Whitehead's wife suffering severe pain. Russell observed that she seemed "cut off from everyone and everything by walls of agony". Russell's own life had been, since his marriage, calm and uncomplicated, but the experience of being with someone suffering extreme pain had a profound effect on Russell. He was led by a train of thoughts to formulate an enduring feeling about human relations:

The loneliness of the human soul is unendurable; nothing can penetrate it except the highest intensity of the sort of love that religious teachers have preached; whatever does not spring from this motive is harmful, or at least useless; it follows that war is wrong, that a public school education is abominable, that the use of force is to be deprecated, and that in human relations one should penetrate to the core of loneliness in each person and speak to that. (Russell, 1951, p. 220)

Russell decided to take Whitehead's son for a walk to protect him and his mother from this moment of pain, and Russell and this boy were close friends until the boy's death in the First World War.

The train of thought that began on that occasion changed Russell radically and permanently. Russell says that at the end of that five minutes, he had become a "completely different person" possessed by a "mystic illumination". He describes his transformation thus:

Having for years cared only for exactness and analysis, I found myself filled with semi-mystical feelings about beauty, with an intense interest in children, and with a desire almost as profound as that of the Buddha to find some philosophy which should make human life endurable. A strange excitement possessed me, containing intense pain but also some element of triumph. . . . The mystic insight which I then imagined myself to possess has largely faded, and the habit of analysis has reasserted itself. But something of what I thought I saw in that moment has always remained with me. (ibid., p. 21)

In this moving episode of Bertrand Russell's life, we can observe the levels of awareness, the several dimensions he travels through in those five minutes and the impact that they leave on his life. It might be quite similar to those intense here and now moments in a group session when the pain of a group member penetrates everybody else in the group and might lead to a significant impact on group members.

From a Lacanian perspective, the intense feeling of empathy that Bertrand Russell feels for Mrs Whitehead, her three-year-old son, and humanity is an example of the register of the Imaginary. It has to do with images and how they convey a totality of feeling and being.

When he starts enunciating a series of convictions that spring spontaneously to his mind during those five minutes of mystic illumination, we have also examples of what Lacan calls the register of

98 THE DIALOGUES IN AND OF THE GROUP

the Symbolic. The symbolic in this case is functioning at the same time that his powerful fantasies create a totality of experience designed to identify with his friends Alfred N. Whitehead and his wife.

When he describes Mrs Whitehead as: "cut off from everyone and everything by walls of agony" and how this affected him, he was witnessing the Real. We can say that in the middle of such encounter, with utmost pain, she can only ex-ist. Russell, on the other hand, responds to this Real with his fantasies and his symbolic codes of value and feels deeply for his friends. To some degree, he is taken by the Real.

However, the encounter is so powerful that he goes into a mystical experience. Russell's mystical illumination is what, in Lacanian terms, we call mystical *jouissance*, a term that indicates both an intense pleasure akin to orgasm, and yet, a liberation from, and mastery over the body. Lacan's concept of mystical *jouissance* is covered especially in his seminar *Encore*, where he deals with feminine sexuality and the mystical experience.

It would seem, then, that mystical experience, and we can extend this to spirituality, requires, from a Lacanian perspective, the courage (another word for spirit) to confront the Real. One needs to take up the chisel and hammer and approach with respect and awe the formless identity of the stone to bring out the many faces of beauty it can reveal.

There is an Other coming from the concrete, unspeakable universe to reveal the human spirit. Russell's confrontation with the outer state of pain in his friend takes him to his own pain, and his great sensitivity enlivened by a rich Imaginary and a vigilant Symbolic enables him to draw from it, like a sculptor, the exquisite symbolic forms of his compassion, his knowledge and his friendship. This is, in my view, an example of moments in a group session where the powers of identification of group members, helped by the symbolic vigilance of the therapist, lead to insight and cultural enrichment.

There is a hunger to be, a want of being that brings people into the psychotherapy group. This is identified by Lacan as desire. It has been named in similar ways by other writers. The Spanish philosopher, José Ortega y Gasset puts it very well:

Man is the hunger to be—the absolute passionate desire to be, to subsist—and the desire to be as he is, to realize his most individual "I." But this has two faces: an entity made up of the desire to be, is evidently

CONCLUSION 99

already in existence; if not, it could not struggle. This on the one hand. But on the other, what is that entity? We have already described it as the eager effort to be. All right; but only he can feel the effort to be who is not quite sure of being, who feels it constantly problematical as to whether he may or may not, in the next moment or so, continue to be, and whether he will be this kind of a being or that. Hence our life is the hunger to be for the very reason that it is at the same time, and at bottom, fundamentally insecure. Hence we are always doing something to assure ourselves of life; and first of all we formulate an interpretation of the environment in which we must have our being and of ourselves as we expect to go on being in it we define the horizon within which we must live. (Ortega y Gasset, 1958, pp. 33–34)

By helping to bring out the animating force in our patients this process becomes mind, will, and feelings, vigour, and courage, it is soul being freed from evil spirits or demons fighting on the side of death against the forces of Eros, life. If this is what psychotherapy is, then there is no doubt in my mind that it is intimately connected with spirituality.

And finally, what is final: death. I have been close to that moment with a few of my patients. There is one that took some time for me and the group to get through.

He came from an island. He was a good swimmer, familiar with the beach. "Francisco" started in a short marital and family psychotherapy.

The marriage ended in divorce. The bulk of the treatment, though, was in individual and group psychotherapy after his divorce. He used to test me quite a bit; he considered me an East Coast type of therapist, very much in need of West Coast influence. He would become quite angry when he felt totally convinced that I had the solution to his problems but was letting him wander aimlessly in search of the answers.

He gradually developed an interest in Jungian psychology and became active in attending workshops and helping others in their personal search through these workshops. In spite of his unabated criticism of my style and orientation, he always professed and maintained in individual and group work an attitude of great respect for me. The transference was full of passion, interest and dogged determination.

Once, in a group session, a woman called his attention to my clumsy interpretation when I commented on the dynamics of his

100   THE DIALOGUES IN AND OF THE GROUP

acting out behaviour. He said to her, "Well, whenever I hear him speak that way, I think, here is a guy that had to take one hundred courses in psychology to get to where he is today. He passed ninety-nine but he flunked one. But hey, what can I say? He passed ninety-nine." To which I then commented, "And you are so unlucky that the one I flunked is the one that applies to you today." Hearing this little dialogue, the group broke into laughter and the anxiety gave way to a more in-depth and compassionate exploration of very difficult and delicate sexual issues in the group.

One day, as he was getting close to terminating his therapy and his life seemed increasingly more rewarding, he told the group members that he was going to miss the following session because he would be attending a Jungian workshop. The workshop was to explore "the dark side" of man. Tragically, he would never return. Two days later I received a message from his former wife. She let me know that Francisco had drowned while saving two group members of his workshop from the rough seas at the beach where he was staying for the workshop. He helped save them, but he was lost in the rough seas and his body was never recovered.

I heard the message many times over the following days, astonished, angry, and terribly sad. I had to tell the group in the following session. The reactions in the group were as varied as the members in it. A woman immediately broke into sobbing and intense grief. One man said that for him what I had just said was simply a phrase that had no meaning for him and that it would take time before he could digest this event. Everybody wanted more information but I had little and we just had to be with ourselves. It took approximately two years for this death to be worked through in the group.

After two years, I invited a new member into the group. About five to six months into the group with this new member, there were a number of comments whereby the memory of "Francisco" started coming back. In this session, I suddenly realised that there was a connection between the new member and the older one. I felt free to talk about my feelings for Francisco and broke into sobbing. The new member found this very meaningful and felt quite connected to the history of this group.

In retrospect, I could see how the new member signalled for the group, and for me, the need to move on and let the death of Francisco inspire us, become a sort of illumination, a presence to overcome the absence, an answer past the question. The work that we had been doing with the Imaginary and the Symbolic functions in the group moved us to draw from the impossible Real a deep spiritual reality. One thing became clear at last: we all in that group, including me, loved Francisco. We could not escape the reality of it, not even the therapist. What kind of love is this? What is the transference and how far does it go? This is a more complex subject for another day. I dare to say that love is what is at the heart of psychotherapy. Is that what the subject of spirituality is leading us to? You all can speak to it.

I dedicate this effort, these wanderings, to the memory of Francisco and all those group members that keep helping me pass course one followed by two zeroes. I keep after the hollowness of those zeroes, out of which I often wish for that invisible that will light up the answers that can defeat all the questions. I know this will not happen. But hey, I already passed ninety-nine courses, don't you think it is worthwhile to keep trying for course one zero zero? Maybe I have to ask Francisco, for I am still at ninety-nine, and he passed one zero zero.

REFERENCES

Bleger, J. (1966). Psychoanalysis of the psychoanalytic frame. *International Journal of Psychoanalysis, 48*: 511–519.

Bleger, J. (1981). Psychoanalysis of the psychoanalytic frame. In: R. Langs (Ed.), *Classics in Psychoanalytic Technique*. New York: Jason Aronson.

Boothby, R. (2001). *Freud as Philosopher: Metapsychology after Lacan*. New York: Routledge.

Borges, J. L. (1967). "Borges and I". In: *A Personal Anthology*, A. Kerrigan (Trans.). New York: Grove Press.

Cassirer, E. (1946). *Language and Myth*. New York: Dover.

Davoine, F., & Gaudilliere, J. M. (2004). *History Beyond Trauma: Whereof One Cannot Speak, Thereof One Cannot Stay Silent*, S. Fairfield (Trans.). New York: Other Press.

de Burgos, J. (1997). *Songs of the Simple Truth: The Complete Poems of Julia de Burgos*, compiled and translated by J. Aguera. Willimantic, CT: Curbstone Press.

Dor, J. (1997). *Introduction to the Reading of Lacan: The Unconscious Structured Like a Language*, J. Feher Gurewich (Ed.), in collaboration with S. Fairfield. Northvale, NJ: Jason Aronson.

Evans, D. (1996). *An Introductory Dictionary of Lacanian Psychoanalysis*. London: Routledge.

REFERENCES   103

Felman, S. (1987). *Jacques Lacan and the Adventure of Insight: Psychoanalysis in Contemporary Culture*. Cambridge, MA: Harvard University Press.

Freud, S. (1900a). *The Interpretation of Dreams*. *S.E.*, 4–5. London: Hogarth.

Freud, S. (1915e). The unconscious. *S.E.*, 14: 161–215. London: Hogarth.

Freud, S. (1920g). *Beyond the Pleasure Principle*. *S.E.*, 18: 7–64. London: Hogarth.

Freud, S. (1930a). *Civilization and its Discontents*. *S.E.*, 21: 59–145. London: Hogarth.

Freud, S. (1950c[1895]). *Project for a Scientific Psychology*. *S.E.*, 1: 283–397. London: Hogarth.

Garaudy, R. (1965). *Les debats de notre temps. De L'Anatheme au Dialogue: Un Marxista Tire les Conclusions du Concile*. Paris: Librairie Plon.

Homer, S. (2005). *Jacques Lacan*. London: Routledge.

Lacan, J. (1947). British psychiatry and the war. *Psychoanalytical Notebooks of the London Circle*, 4: 9–34..

Lacan, J. (1949). The mirror stage as formative of the function of the I as revealed in psychoanalytic experience. In: *Ecrits, A Selection*, A. Sheridan (Trans.). London: Routledge/Tavistock.

Lacan, J. (1953–1954). *The Seminar of Jacque Lacan, Book I: Freud's Papers on Technique*. New York: Norton, 1991.

Lacan, J. (1954–1955). *The Seminar of Jacques Lacan, Book II: The Ego in Freud's Theory and in the Technique of Psychoanalysis*, J.-A. Miller (Ed.), S. Tomaselli (Trans.) with notes by John Forrester. New York: Norton, 1988.

Lacan, J. (1955–1956). *Seminar Book III. The Psychoses*, J.-A. Miller (Ed.), R. Grigg (Trans.). New York: Norton, 1993.

Lacan, J. (1964). *The Four Fundamental Concepts of Psychoanalysis*. J.-A Miller (Ed.). Translated by A. Sheridan, New York: Norton. (1978).

Lacan, J. (1966). *Ecrits: A Selection*, A. Sheridan (Trans.). Paris: Editions du Seuil. New York: W. W. Norton, 1977.

Lacan, J. (1974–1975). R.S.I. text established by Jacques-Alain Miller. *Ornicar?*, 2 (1975): 87–105; 3(1975): 95–110; 4(1975): 91–106; 5(1975): 15–66. One class translated by Jacqueline Ross in Feminine Sexuality, 162–171.

Lacan, J. (1975). *The Seminar of Jacques Lacan, Book XX: Encore, On Feminine Sexuality, The Limits of Love and Knowledge 1972–73*, J.-A. Miller (Ed.), B. Fink (Trans.). New York: Norton, 1998.

Lacan, J. (1978). *Seminar XI, The Four Fundamental Concepts of Psychoanalysis*, J.-A. Miller (Ed.), A. Sheridan (Trans.). New York: W. W. Norton.

104 REFERENCES

Leiber, J., & Stoller, L. (1968). *Is That All There Is?* Milwaukee: Hal Leonard.

Miller, J.-A. (1995). Introductory talk at Sainte-Anne Hospital. In: R. Feldstein, B. Fink, & M. Jaanus (Eds.), *Reading Seminar XI: Lacan's Four Fundamental Concepts of Psychoanalysis* (pp. 233–242). Albany, NY: State University of New York Press.

Miller, J.-A. (1996). An introduction to Seminars I and II. In: R. Feldstein, B. Fink, & M. Jaanus (Eds.), *Reading Seminars I and II. Lacan's Return to Freud* (pp. 3–36). Albany, NY: State University of New York Press.

Ortega y Gasset, J. (1958). *Man and Crisis*. New York: W. W. Norton.

Roudinesco. E. (1997). *Jacques Lacan*. New York: Columbia University Press.

Russell, B. (1951). *The Autobiography of Bertrand Russell*. Boston, MA: Little Brown, 1967.

Saussure, F. de (1966). *Course in General Linguistics*, C. Bally & Albert Jechehaye with A. Reidlinger (Eds.), W. Baskin (Trans.). New York: McGraw Hill.

Scott Lee, J. (1990). *Jacques Lacan*. Amherst, MA: University of Massachusetts Press.

Soler, C. (1995). The subject and the other (I). In: R. Feldstein, B. Fink, & M. Jaanus (Eds.), *Reading Seminar XI: Lacan's Four Fundamental Concepts of Psychoanalysis* (pp. 45–54). Albany, NY: State University of New York Press.

Teilhard de Chardin, P. (1926–1927). *The Divine Milieu*. New York: Harper Perennial Modern Classics, 2001.

Teilhard de Chardin, P. (1938–1940). *The Phenomenon of Man*. New York: Harper Perennial Modern Classics, 2008.

Winnicott, D. W. (1971). The use of an object and relating through identifications. In: *Playing and Reality* (pp. 86–94). New York: Penguin, 1990.

Winnicott, D. W. (1975). *Through Pediatrics to Psychoanalysis*. New York: Basic Books.

INDEX

Abbaye de Hautecombe, 4
alienation, 64, 78, 81–83, 86–88
Althusser, L., 7
American Group Psychotherapy
    Association (AGPA), xvi–xvii,
    49, 91, 95
anger, 29, 35–36, 47, 49, 53, 56, 68, 73,
    75–77, 80, 83, 99–100
anxiety, x, xiv, 31, 35–36, 42, 48–49,
    55–57, 61–62, 65–66, 68, 77, 93,
    100
    acute, 4
    group, 43
    social, 27

Baruzi, J., 4
behaviour, 10, 54, 56, 61, 63, 66, 92,
    100
    hostile, 77
    symbolic, 14
Benedictine, 4–5
Bion, W. R., ix, xiv, 6, 14–15
Bleger, J., 66, 102

Boothby, R., 20, 102
Borges, J. L., 32–33, 102
Borromean Knot, 15
Braudel, F., 7

Case studies
    Adelle, 53–54, 56, 63, 68
    Alvaro, 53–54, 57, 63, 67
    Andrew, 71–77, 79–86
    Arcadia, 53–54, 56, 62
    Belinda, 53–55, 63
    Bernie, 26–27, 31–32
    Brent, 26–28, 31
    Carla, 72, 75, 77, 85
    Catalina, 26
    Chris, 72, 74–75, 77, 85
    Donna, 26, 29
    Francisco, 99–101
    Gina, 71–75, 77, 79–81, 83, 85
    Jonathan, 53–57, 63, 67, 72, 74–77, 85
    Julia, 53–57, 62
    Leonard, 72–77, 84–85
    Marie, 72–73, 75, 77, 85

106 INDEX

Matilde, 47–48
Mitra, 72–74, 77, 80, 85, 88
Ortensia, 53–54, 56, 63, 66
Paul, 28, 31
Robert, 72, 74–75, 77
Rodino, 26, 28–31
Rodrigo, 53–57, 62–63, 67–68
Sandra, 72, 77
Stanford, 53, 55, 63, 65, 67–68
Yolanda, 26, 29
Cassirer, E., 44, 102
Catholic University, Washington,
    DC, x
Christian Brothers (Frères des Ecoles
    Chrétiennes), x
College Stanislas, 4
Columbia University, 7
Columbian Congress, x
Colombian National Academy of
    History, x
conscious(ness), 9–10, 14, 19, 31, 69
    see also: unconscious(ness)
    pre-, 10

Dali, S., 5
Davoine, F., xv, 102
death, xiv, xvii, 49, 57, 62, 65, 68,
    75–76, 79, 83, 96–97, 99–100
    drive, 12
    fear of, 49
    psychic, 81
de Burgos, J., 70, 102
de Gaulle, C., 4
development(al), 6, 20, 24, 38–39,
    42–43, 45, 50, 66, 69, 81, 84, 95
    language, 64
    theoretical, 12
Dor, J., 17–18, 45, 102

Ecole de la cause freudienne, 8
Ecole des Hautes Etudes, Paris, xv,
    5
Ecole Française de Paris (EFP), 7–8
Ecole Française de psychanalyse
    (EFP), 7
Ecole Normale Supérieure, 7–8

ego, ix, xviii, 5–6, 9–10, 12, 16–19,
    21–22, 31, 41, 47, 64–66, 70, 94
    alter, 18, 41
    ideal, 55
    meta-, 66
    narrative, 10, 34
    psychology, 5, 36, 85, 95
    super-, 10, 55
Evans, D., 10, 84, 102

fantasy, 17, 19, 24–25, 82, 88
Felman, S., 69, 103
Fondation du Champ Freudien, 8
Frank, J., 118
Freud, S., ix, xiii–xiv, xvii–xviii, 3,
    5–8, 10–13, 16, 18, 20, 22–23,
    36–38, 45–46, 50, 64, 69, 78,
    85–86, 88, 91–93, 95, 103
    Rat Man, 13

Garaudy, R., x, 94, 103
Gaudilliere, J. M., xv, 102
Georgetown University, x

Hartman, H., 6
Homer, S., 8, 42, 103
Hôpital Sainte Anne, 5

International Psychoanalytic
    Association (IPA), 7, 10, 14

Jakobson, R., 36, 38
James, C., xi
Johns Hopkins University, 7
Jung, C. G., 99–100

Kojeve, A., 5–6

Lacan, J., ix, xi, xiii–xviii, 3–21, 23–25,
    29–30, 32, 36, 38–39, 41–51, 55,
    63–64, 66–67, 69–70, 78, 81–82,
    84–88, 91, 95–98, 103
    Trilogy
        Imaginary, xi, xvi–xvii, 9, 18–20,
            22, 47–48, 52, 55, 64, 95,
            97–98, 101

INDEX 107

Real, xi, xvii, 12, 18, 36, 40, 42, 48, 52, 80, 84, 95–96, 98, 101
Symbolic, xi, xvi–xvii, 11, 18–20, 22, 48, 55, 64, 76, 80, 95–96, 98, 101
Leiber, J., 90, 104
Levi-Strauss, C., 36, 38
life, xvi, 4, 8, 12, 17, 25–26, 29, 33, 35, 43, 53–54, 62, 65, 69, 75–76, 81–83, 92–93, 96–97, 99–100
adult, 50
drive, 12
early, 12, 20, 29
emotional, 88
human, 92, 97
love, 77
professional, xiv, 36, 91
Lowenstein, R., 5–6

Massachusetts Institute of Technology, 7
McDougall, J., xv
memory, xv, 4, 45, 100–101
Miller, J.-A., 7–8, 14, 69, 86, 104
mOther, 17, 40, 81
mother, ix, 12, 16–18, 31, 40, 45–47, 62, 64–65, 72–73, 75–77, 81, 95, 97
child–, 30
god-, 49

National Group Psychotherapy Institute, xv
New International Library of Group Analysis (NILGA), ix
Northfield centre, 14

object, 9–11, 15, 17, 20, 27, 30, 37, 42, 45–47, 49, 82, 84–85
imaginary, 10
lost, ix, 15, 20, 30, 47
partial, 24–25
physical, 45
relations, ix, xvi, xviii, 36, 42–43, 48, 85, 91, 95–96
transitional, 50

Ortega y Gasset, J., 96, 98–99, 103
Other, 11–12, 16, 18–19, 30–31, 39–41, 43–44, 46–48, 64, 67–68, 70, 78, 81–83, 85–88, 96, 98

parent(s), x, 12, 17, 30, 66, 74–75, 77, 85, 88
Pines, M., xi
psychosis, xv, 12, 42, 81, 83
paranoiac, 5

repression, 18, 21, 25, 43, 47, 55, 65, 76, 85
Rickman, J., ix, xiv, 14
Riollano, M., xi
Roudinesco, E., xvi, 4–6, 104
Russell, B., xvii, 96–98, 104

Saussure, F. de, 36–39, 104
Scott Lee, J., 14, 104
self, ix, 17, 61, 66, 70
-aware(ness), 6
-deceptive, 69
psychology, xviii, 85, 91, 96
separation, 32, 78, 81–82, 86–88
sexual, 22, 26, 42, 100
desire, 26
drive, 26–27
experience, 42
frustrations, 26
identity, 62
jouissance, 43
pleasure, 84
psycho-, 8
trauma, 43
sexuality, 26
feminine, 98
signifier, 10, 12–13, 17–19, 22, 31–32, 36–37, 39–41, 43, 49, 51, 69, 80–83, 85–88
absent, 12
central, 12
key, 11, 13, 96
main, 25, 83
master, 82, 87
primary, 82

108 INDEX

repressed, 43, 76
unary, 32
Societé Française de Psychanalyse
(SFP), 7
Societé Psychanalitique de Paris
(SPP), 5
Soler, C., 81, 86, 104
Stoller, L., 90, 104
subject(s), xvi, xviii, 5, 10, 12, 14, 16,
18–19, 22, 25, 29–30, 32, 41–47,
49, 64, 78, 81–82, 84–88, 95–96
Cartesian, xvii, 67, 78, 86
Freudian, 78, 86
Lacanian, xvii
neurotic, 79
subjectivity, 17–18, 36, 82, 91
inter-, 41, 70

Teilhard de Chardin, P., x, 94, 104
transference, xi, xvi, xviii, 9, 14, 25,
29–30, 36, 45, 62, 65–66, 68, 78,
99, 101
counter-, xi
horizontal, 11, 19, 62

imaginary, 80
vertical, 19, 62, 80

unconscious(ness), ix, xiv, xvii–xviii,
3–4, 8, 10, 12–14, 16, 18–19,
21–22, 25, 32, 36–38, 40, 42–44,
51–52, 61, 63–69, 78–80, 85–86,
88, 94–95 see also: conscious(ness)
Freudian, 69
repressed, 11
social, xi
University of Paris-Vincennes, 7

Von Humboldt, A. W., 44

war, xiv, 7, 14, 97
First World, 4, 97
Second World, 6, 29
Washington School of Psychiatry, xi,
xiv–xvi, 49
Winnicott, D. W., ix, xv, 49–50, 65,
104

Yale University, 7